MORE DECORATING WITH

FLOWERS

MORE DECORATING WITH
FLOWERS

by Ronaldo Maia

Denise Otis, Consulting Editor

❧

ABRADALE PRESS

HARRY N. ABRAMS, INC., PUBLISHERS

Editor: Margaret L. Kaplan

Designer: Dana Sloan

Library of Congress Cataloging-in-Publication Data
Maia, Ronaldo.
More decorating with flowers / by Ronaldo Maia ;
Denise Otis, consulting editor.
p.   cm.
Includes index.
ISBN 0–8109–8141–6
1. Flower arrangement.   2. Flower arrangement—
Pictorial works.   3. Entertaining.
I. Otis, Denise.   II. Title.
SB449.M324   1995   95–2340
745.92—dc20   CIP

To Nature,

the mother of my inspiration

◊

To my family,

the source of my values

◊

To my sister,

Maria Paulina Pezzi Maia Teixeira,

who taught me the

full meaning of brotherhood

◊

To New York,

that diamond-like city—

hard, brilliant, irreplaceable

◊

To my very special friend

and colleague,

James Abbott O'Brien

◊

To all the friends and clients

who have supported me

◊

To the beauty of flowers

CONTENTS

INTRODUCTION

AND

ACKNOWLEDGMENTS

8

AT HOME

WITH

FLOWERS

14

FLOWER

ARRANGING

AS AN

ART FORM

36

FLOWERS

FOR THE

TABLE

58

PARTY FLOWERS—

ARRANGEMENTS

ON A

GRAND SCALE

76

FLOWERS

FOR THE

WEDDING

104

CONTAINERS

FROM

NATURE

142

DESIGNS FOR

THE HOLIDAY

SEASON

158

STYLE,

ORIGINALITY,

SURPRISE

182

INDEX

211

❧

Swagging or hanging garlands on lighting fixtures puts flowers at the eye level of standing guests. See also page 96.

Many years ago I read three precepts for an accomplished life proposed by a great man. I have long since forgotten the man's name, but I have always remembered his precepts: to plant a tree, to have a child, to write a book.

When I was still a child I planted my first tree. It grew so fast that soon I could climb its branches to see the world from its top. It was a friend. And I still plant trees whenever I have the opportunity.

My children are the people I have taught to arrange flowers. Those who have worked for me and gone on to start their own businesses, those who have come to my lectures and demonstrations, those whose way of seeing and fixing flowers I have influenced—all of them I consider my children.

For my book *Decorating with Flowers* it was my very great pleasure to have as co-authors Denise Otis, who wrote the text, and Ernst Beadle, who took the photographs. I am very proud of our creation.

But I have added one more precept: Never stop creating. If one is open to them, there are always new challenges and new inspirations—new ideas, new materials, new flowers to try. Over the last few years I have commissioned photographs of arrangements that I particularly liked. This book is a collection

of those photographs, taken by a variety of distinguished photographers. Some arrangements that stayed in my mind after they were completed but were not photographed in the rush of a deadline, I have re-created, or, where this was not possible, have tried to describe.

The range of flowers and leaves and grasses available to florists has increased enormously in the last ten years. For many years it was almost impossible to find sweet peas—now they are back and in many colors. Montecassino asters, goldenrod, sunflowers, and a variety of grasses now bring the meadow to the corner flower shop. American wildflowers like lisianthus and godetia, their size and stamina improved by plant breeders, are also newcomers. And more and more highly unusual flowers from Australia, New Zealand, South Africa, and South America have appeared on the scene. To take advantage of all these newly available materials, however, a florist must seek out new suppliers. Not all florists are motivated to do so or are even aware that such suppliers and such materials exist.

If you cannot find the materials I have used in a particular arrangement, there are several strategies that you can pursue. You can encourage your local florist to obtain those leaves or flowers or grasses—requests from a steady and valued client are highly motivating. If you live where you can have a garden—often city dwellers can't—you can grow many of them yourself. Which plants your garden can produce will depend on the part of the country in which you live. Or you can study the colors and textures carefully and substitute other leaves or flowers to create a similar if not identical effect. I love galax leaves, for example, and use them in a great many of my arrangements. A florist should be able to get them for you, but if he can't or won't, some possible substitutes are the leaves of geranium or the lacier ones of rose geranium, of hosta which is not quite as round but comes in many shades of green, *Ricinus communis* (the castor oil plant), even delphinium; but all are less shiny than galax. A glossier stand-in might be the leaves of *Fatsia japonica,* which is often available as a houseplant. But, to put in a last word for my favorite, none of these are as long-lasting as galax, which can be used over and over again.

In this book I have devoted considerable space to the discussion of decorations for weddings and large parties, and not all of this discussion is about flowers. The experience of designing many such celebrations in the dozen or so years since *Decorating with Flowers* was published has taught me many useful strategems for making big parties run smoothly, information that I have not seen in other books and would like to share. If you know how to prevent uncomfortable situations from developing, you can plan your festivities more intelligently, whether you are organizing them yourself, or working with a volunteer committee or professional party planner. And you as well as your guests will be free to really enjoy the party.

Although I may use lights and fabrics and lattices in party decorations, it is plants and flowers that I most love and most love to work with. I believe that seeing and living with flowers every day helps us learn to love Nature and to understand that, following Nature's rule, we must replace and replenish what we take from Nature in order to preserve our environment. I hope in these pages to inspire you with the same love of flowers that has made my professional life so happy.

No one works alone, and I would like to express my appreciation to those who have helped me and who have made so many contributions to this book. Setsuo

❦

A posy of roses, freesia, sweet

peas, and Queen Anne's lace. See

also page 68.

Kitano, brother in taste and a very special talent, Anderson Costa, for the care he takes in handling, and the late Michael Mickoseff, whom we all miss. I would also like to thank all those extra hands and supporters: Lorraine O'Brien, Luis Casanas, Audrey Schwartzberg, and Sagrario Perez-Soto. And all the remarkable photographers whose work appears on these pages: Jade Albert, Fernando Bengoechea, Roger Bester, Edgar DeEvia, Fred Marcus, Mick Hales, Marisa Alves Lima, Peter Margonelli, Joseph Mehling, Julio Piedra, Eric Weiss, and the Skelton Studio in San Francisco (for Gump's). I have been blessed with many loyal and supportive clients, and would particularly like to thank those who have allowed me to photograph their houses and apartments and parties—Ms. Lourdes Catão, Mr. and Mrs. Gordon Getty, Ms. Jan Maakestad, Mrs. Paige Rense, Mrs. Lyn Revson, Mme Walter Moreira Salles, Mr. and Mrs. Irving Schloss, Mr. and Mrs. Fernan Vargas, Mrs. Robert Wales, Mrs. John Hay Whitney, and The Kips Bay Boys' & Girls' Club—as well as the families, brides, grooms, and bridesmaids who have lent me their wedding pictures—Mr. and Mrs. Ray Treiger, Betsy Shuster, Mr. and Mrs. Lauren F. Otis, Dr. and Mrs. Max Ots, Ms. Mary Marks, Mrs. Anson Nolen, Mrs. Naomi Klarner, Mrs. Sagrario Perez-Soto. I would also like to express my gratitude to my editor, Margaret Kaplan, and especially to my consulting editor and good friend Denise Otis, who has so generously shared her knowledge, wisdom, and style.

❦

A big bouquet of flowers in the entrance hall welcomes and lifts the spirits of everyone who comes through the front door. This arrangement stands well over three feet tall in its faux-porphyry urn and is raised another foot above the hall's center table by a faux-marble cube. White lilies and the tiny white cultivated asters called Montecassino asters or September weed by florists are punctuated with plumes of pennisetum, also called fountain grass. A similar arrangement using native wild asters and meadow grasses would probably be smaller in scale, for cultivation lengthens stems. Photograph by Peter Margonelli.

One day someone asked me if I really thought it was important to have flowers in the house. At first I had no answer: It is hard to imagine a home with no soul.

Flowers in the house, for me, are as important as light. Sharing your life with nature in any way, even one as simple as cut flowers in the house, is not only important but essential.

This is something that children seem to know instinctively. A little child finds it very difficult to understand why he cannot pick and take home any blossom that happens to catch his fancy, not to speak of any toad or frog or insect he happens to catch. Probably most parents would prefer the stolen flower even if it does mean apologies to a neighboring gardener. And we should not dismiss with a glance that bouquet of weeds from the roadside offered up by grubby little hands. If we looked at each of those weeds with the attention we give to a balance sheet or a painting, we might be able to see again the beauty and interest that the child finds in every detail of the natural world.

Living with flowers is not a complicated or expensive or time-consuming way to nourish our ties to nature. The flowers need not be abundant or rare or carefully arranged. Such refinements are certainly enjoyable, but are they any more enjoyable than simplicity? A dozen scarlet tulips standing straight and even in a cube of crystal, then growing and bending and

❦

For a quiet afternoon tea with a
good friend, a Russian metal table
painted to imitate *pietra dura* work
holds a silver Versailles box of
nerines and freesia accented with
wavy spikes of blue veronica. The
Victorian slipper chairs are
English, and the mirror as well as
the carved and gilded wooden
bracket and flower vases over the
bed are Dutch eighteenth century.
The bedroom was decorated by
James O'Brien. Photograph by
Guy Lindsay

bowing as the days go by. Three fat pink peonies. A pottery pitcher gathering in an autumn field of goldenrod and starry blue and white asters.

True, flowers have very short lives. But that enables them to bring another gift to the house, the gift of continual refreshment. If a rose lasted for months, it would become a fixed part of the decoration and we would cease to see it. In the few days that it passes from bud to blossom to petals on the table it keeps us fascinated with its subtle changes of form and color. And each different flower or arrangement of flowers alters the way we look at the objects near it. A spray of white lilies underlines the formal purity of a collection of celadon; a bowl of fragile fluffy white sweet peas calls attention by contrast to the taffy-gloss texture of the glaze. And we all have our favorite memories of the way flowers in an unexpected color have made us see a painting or a piece of fabric or a porcelain jar in a whole new light. Perhaps to live with flowers is all we need do to be reborn each day with new eyes so that we may be surprised anew with the beauty of things—and people—to which custom has blinded us.

The place for flowers in a house is any place that you choose, near things that you love and wish to honor, or where they will bring you joy or comfort. You probably won't always choose the same place, at least if you love all the variety of flowers. Finding a balance between the space that will be occupied by the flowers and the flowers themselves is important. There is just enough room on the table with the silver box collection to tuck in a bud vase with a handful of violets or a single rose or a few sprigs of heather: anything larger and the boxes would have to be put away for a while—not always a bad idea. Single flowers or little bud-vase bouquets are the easiest to place in a room: they don't pretend to make statements. They simply offer a touch of living color for tranquil contemplation.

"Flaming Parrot" tulips, their long stems clasped in a tall glass cylinder, swirl and bend in front of a severe Dutch eighteenth-century carved ebony mirror. The arrangement is very simple—cut a few of the stems in varied lengths and the tulips will do the rest. The choice of color seems daring, but the fiery featherings of yellow and carmine glow against the raspberry-sherbet walls of this small sitting room designed by James O'Brien. A Japanese bronze monk and a Thai lacquer frog-on-a-box join the tulips on the chest of drawers, which was given a faux-jasper finish to harmonize with the marbelized mantel. In the foreground, a nineteenth-century Jacobean Revival cane and mahogany chair on an antique Portuguese needlepoint rug. Next to the globe on the little tray-table is a *penca de balangandas*, the collection of silver pomegranates, melons, coins, and other good luck charms worn by the women of Bahia in northern Brazil on a silver chain around the waist.

Photographs by Guy Lindsay.

The tapestry-cushioned stool facing the fireplace in another view of the same tiny sitting room might have been the brainchild of a Cubist, but it is in fact a nineteenth-century English grotto seat. A small cactus-wood table holds books beside the seventeenth-century Brazilian Dutch Colonial jacaranda-wood desk. The cottage Victorian ebony armchair is upholstered in white canvas. A contemporary Brazilian folk-art dog crouches on the hearth in front of the marbelized wooden mantelpiece. Over it hangs a composition of eighteenth- and early nineteenth-century miniatures, and between the windows a daguerreotype is suspended on a suede ribbon. A smaller *penca de balangandas* gets pink highlights from the desk-top mixed bouquet of tulips, lilacs, viburnum, and pale and rose-pink amaryllis in a container wrapped in a pouf of striped chintz. What looks like a red feather duster under the desk is a single dried stem of scarlet *celosia cristata*.

An arrangement of fruit and flowers that effectively complements a painting by William Sheets without trying to duplicate exactly the painting's specific subjects, which is rarely possible—or successful even when possible. One would be hard put to identify these painted blossoms, but the pink and white peonies in the repoussé silver pitcher echo their forms and textures. Some of the colors and the solid rotundity of the forms are repeated at a considerably smaller scale in the bowl of grapes, Spanish cherries, baby eggplant, and ripe prickly pears. Photograph by Fernando Bengoechea.

Larger bouquets, even if they are simple and casual, ask for more consideration. You may have a special spot where you usually place flowers. Most of us do. Then someone gives you an arrangement or you fall in love with a kind of flower that just doesn't fit in that space. A basket of zinnias is perfect on the coffee table but the tall cobalt glass cylinder that holds lilacs or lilies so gracefully is too tall and looks better on the window sill or the console under the mirror. I'm always grateful for the push to experiment. Just trying out a vase of flowers in different places in a room often suggests new and interesting ways to rearrange objects or even furniture.

Flowers soften the hard edges and brighten the dark corners of a house. Tall branches of blooming quince or forsythia, or of scarlet maple leaves, sheaves of reeds or pampas grass will bring to life a bare corner that may lack sufficient light and air circulation to support a living tree. And we ought to revive the old custom of filling the hearth with flowers during warm weather. Armloads of lilacs, or peonies or Queen Anne's Lace usually do not cost much when they are in season; but if flowers of the right size and color are difficult or expensive to come by in sufficient quantity, a big bouquet of long-lasting green leaves is just as beautiful and sometimes even more refreshing. A few flowers tucked in from time to time will give it spice.

When we give flowers a proper setting in our rooms we give ourselves a series of living pictures throughout the year. But flowers at home have still another pleasure to offer, the pleasure of scent. Scent in a room is like a flower in a lapel—the finishing touch.

Of course, not all flowers can perfume a room, and in fact some of the most highly scented—roses and carnations—when greenhouse-grown give off at best only a ghost of their natural fragrance. And they are the only roses and carnations available to us unless we grow our own or have generous friends with gardens. Still, we can almost always find narcissus, hyacinths, freesia, some lilies, stock, and sometimes the less common but even more heady jasmine, stephanotis, gardenia, and flowering ginger. To these we can add fragrant fruit and all the pungent and sweet-smelling herbs. Some that I love: in the heat of summer, a bowl of oranges; in the cold of winter, cloves and cinnamon; in spring, lavender; and in autumn, apples.

Fortunately, we don't have to depend on fresh flowers and fruit to give our rooms that finishing touch; we have their fragrances captured in essential oils and blended into more complex scents: potpourris and what I like to call *parfums d'ambiance*. One of

❧

Deep blue delphinium and glowing green euphorbia, probably *Euphorbia palustris*, make a vibrant bouquet for a hall table. Joining the rich harmony, a mound of grapes and a single dark red dahlia are borne aloft by a pair of Victorian Venetian blackamoors. A French Empire bench adds a light touch to the stripe-upholstered walls of this small entrance hall designed by James O'Brien. Photograph by Guy Lindsay

the nicest attentions to the comfort of a guest room—along with the books, flowers, fruits and all the little practical supplies—is to air and spray lightly the closets and drawers so when they are opened they do not smell of past years or moth balls.

One caution. A house, like a person, should stick to one scent at a time. It is very hard to combine successfully all the different notes of several different potpourris or *parfums d'ambiance*. In fact, when you have strongly scented flowers in a room it is a good idea to retire the potpourri bowl, unless the essence of that flower happens to be one of the elements in the potpourri.

Often small gestures open large doors of feeling. Sometimes in the morning we feel blue, but not for long if there's a flower on the night table or next to the bathtub to look at you when you wake up. And one flower on a breakfast table—or tray if we are very lucky—will warm up the heart and fill the eyes with beauty.

Flowers do so much for us that we should be most careful to respect their needs—for water and light, for protection from dryness and drafts and from too much heat or cold.

Making flowers look their best and last their longest begins with proper preparation. The stems should be cut on a long slanting angle using a good sharp knife, whether you are cutting from the plant or recutting flowers from the florist. Boughs from shrubs and trees with tough woody stems—lilacs, dogwood, mock orange, quince, forsythia, to mention a few—usually last longer when you also slit the stems and remove most of the leaves. After cutting, stems should go immediately into water.

If you cut from a garden or pick in a meadow, do so early in the morning or at the end of the day, never in the heat of midday. If possible, take along a container of water

🐦

Frankly contrived topiary balls on birch-branch stems show to advantage the rich tones and velvety texture of cockscomb celosia. A welcome source of color in the garden from the middle of summer until frost, *Celosia cristata* is not easy to use in a loose or informal arrangement because the stem is generally very thick and stiff and the large flowerhead—in some cultivars it can measure ten inches by six inches—does not have a very graceful underpinning. However, celosia comes into its own in rather tightly packed mass arrangements, and is particular suited to topiary fantasies as the blossoms dry very well, keeping their color all winter. Topiaries are right at home in the very eighteenth-century atmosphere evoked by the Rococo swirls of the mirror and the Louis XV chinoiserie lacquer commode, the turquoise-glazed Chinese geese, the ormolu-mounted Chinese vase, and the collection of gold boxes and *objets de vertu* in a living room decorated by Lourdes Catão. Photograph by Guy Lindsay.

so that the flowers can go right in. Just as soon as you get back to the house you should give those flowers a good conditioning. It is not possible to stress too much the value of conditioning.

Almost all flowers, those you buy as well as those you cut, benefit from conditioning. I've found that for the great majority the simplest and most effective conditioning is to let them sit, if possible in a cool dark place, for anywhere from a few minutes to a half hour in warm water, water that feels good and warm to your hand, before you start to arrange them. Many times this will even revive flowers that seem hopelessly wilted—flowers can be born again, too.

Then, when you start to arrange the flowers, be sure to remove all the leaves that will be under or even touching the water. The soft tissue of the leaf decays quickly in water and shortens the life of the flower.

If I am ending this chapter on a practical note, it is because the basic preparation that makes flowers at home in our lives is also the first step in the art of arranging them.

*F*our variations on a theme for winter: niche arrangements of *Hydrangea paniculata* 'Grandiflora', popularly called the PeeGee hydrangea. Flower-bearing branches stripped of their leaves can be arranged fresh and will keep their shape and their heads up while drying in the container.

❧

A starfish inspires a lively composition rising from a moss-covered container. In one incarnation, opposite, the hydrangeas are accompanied solely by a fringe of soft mauve caspia, *Limonium bellidifolium*. Above, white orchids, pink rosebuds, and a constellation of pink and white lilies offer a more colorful variation. All photographs by Peter Margonelli.

❧

If you wish to add fresh flowers to a dried arrangement, you need a supply of florist's water picks, or failing those, test tubes, but the latter are considerably more difficult to handle. In this design, a curvy triangle is spangled with white freesia, white dendrobium orchids, and a few pink lilies.

❧

In a variation on the shape, the addition of three salmon-pink gerbera gives punch to the very subtle combination.

In winning and light-hearted contrast to a red-and-black chinoiserie lacquer console and a heavily carved and gilded mirror, a low box of daisies and galax leaves, set in florist's foam, and a pair of saucy hand-painted Costa Rican wooden parrots brighten up a small entrance hall. Proof if proof were needed that serious furnishings don't always have to have serious flowers. Photograph by Roger Bester.

Flowers to view from above: Two red roses, a pink peony and a red-flecked white one anchor the center of a square basket filled with fragrant sweet peas in shades of pink, mauve, and violet with a sprinkling of white. Flower stems are cut short and fixed in florist's foam, concealed by a few well-placed galax leaves, in the basket's metal liner. Cutting short the stem doesn't hurt the flower—it may even make it last longer—and is often crucial to the achievement of pleasing proportions. Be fearless. Here the basket almost fills the surface of a small square table—a pair might flank a sofa for a party—but it would be perfect for a coffee table, where tall arrangements almost always look awkward or precarious. Photograph by Fernando Bengoechea.

Only the minuscule size of the Versailles box it is "planted" in gives away the fact that this unsheared standard boxwood was not grown but constructed from branch tips set in a wire sphere filled with florist's foam. A living standard, a plant pruned to a single stem in imitation of a tree—Swedish myrtle, bay, rosemary, lavender, and lemon verbena are among the possibilities—would not only need a larger pot or box to accommodate its roots; it would also have to live in daylight or under special plant lights most of the time. Otherwise its lifespan would differ little from that of the constructed kind. Sharing the top of the Rococo table are a gilt and silver Indian lion and bird, and an arrangement of lilies and grapes, hydrangeas and roses, scabiosa and sweet peas in an oval galax-clad container. The painting in the background is by Fred Weymer. Photograph by Guy Lindsay.

A trove of treasures for the eye
includes a noble Tang Dynasty
stallion flanked by polychrome
contemporaries and their riders on
roof tiles, a pair of Chinese export
famille rose porcelain platters, a
silver-mounted coconut, an ornate
Portuguese silver incense burner,
and an eighteenth-century gilt
bronze Thai deity. Two bouquets
of flowers add still more color to
the objects composed by Lourdes
Catão on a Louis XVI giltwood
console table: in the foreground a
seemingly artless bunch of
bachelor's buttons; on the table a
twig basket with a mixture of lilies,
tiny asters, goldenrod, scented
Eucomis autumnalis or pineapple
flower, and clusters of polyantha
roses circling a sheaf of wheat.
Photograph by Guy Lindsay.

A sitting room table set up to scent an apartment for a festive dinner. Sprays of white dendrobium orchids arch over an antique Persian bowl filled with floating lily blossoms. Silver candlesticks and sugar dredgers mingle with a collection of smaller Persian pottery bowls, also antique, holding potpourri and incense sticks, and at the back of the table three glass flasks present three stems of star-of-Bethlehem. Photograph by Marisa Alvarez Lima.

Lights, color, fragrance—an assembly of exotica in a potpourri-filled ceremonial lacquer bowl with a baluster pedestal from Thailand. A glittering Tibetan wedding headdress is perched on a carved gourd; one glass flask displays a mahogany cypripedium orchid, the other, three scarlet ixora clusters; the serpent in this Eden, a Tibetan horn fitted with a silver dragon's head. Photograph by Marisa Alvarez Lima.

Fresh but discreet touch for a small space between two doors, a lined wire basket holds a red, white, and green bouquet of strawberries, sweet peas, and galax leaves on a small console borne by an eighteenth-century Italian wooden angel. The strawberries are impaled on thin bamboo skewers and anchored in florist's foam. Galax-wrapped votive candles cast subtle highlights on the surrounding Chinese objets d'art—porcelain plates, an enameled bird on a malachite slab, and a melon-shaped enamel bowl. The early nineteenth century still life is by the Brazilian painter Bicho, and the apartment was decorated by Lourdes Catão. Photograph by Guy Lindsay.

❦

Mounded in an oval silver bowl, a soft mosaic of blossoms—lilies, peonies, tea roses, clusters of miniature roses, and sweet peas—is rewarding to the eye but not competitive with the vista of lawn and trees, harbor and sailboats beyond the library window. Whenever flowers will be seen against a complex background, whether it be a landscape or a strong pattern in fabric or wallpaper, a massed design with a simple silhouette usually is more agreeable than a linear one, in which the spaces between flowers are as important as the flowers themselves. Photograph by Fernando Bengoechea.

❦

Flowers to wake up with, a tussie-mussie of roses, rosebuds, and pale pink nerines swirled with galax leaves on the bedside table echoes the charm if not the exact mix of blossoms of the flower print on the bedroom wall of an apartment decorated by James O'Brien. Tussie-mussie is the Victorian name for a packed bouquet. Photograph by Guy Lindsay

A small informal gathering of buds and blossoms in a dark-stained split bamboo basket gives each flower "nodding room." Above the variegated pink rose resting on the basket's rim, four apricot roses, tightly budded to full-blown, mingle with wine-dark sweet peas, a blue lace flower, and furry poppy buds. As cut flowers, poppies require special treatment: the cut must be immediately seared with flame or dipped in boiling water to keep the milky sap in just the cells where it belongs and prevent it from filling and sealing the whole stem, thus cutting off the flower's water supply. Photograph courtesy of Gumps.

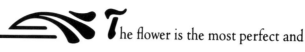

The flower is the most perfect and fragile work of art given to us. Nature has put as much artistry and refinement into a single flower as Fabergé did into an Easter egg, and a single flower richly deserves a place among the precious objects that we collect and display in our houses. For me a single flower is the ultimate encounter of simplicity and luxury.

I like to design with single flowers alone or in groups with each in its individual container. Then you can see each flower with space around it. I may arrange several to create the look of a meadow in spring with blooms popping up here and there. I may lay them out in geometric or free designs on a tabletop or place them around objects—nodding to a figurine, ringing an antique tureen, weaving garlands around candlesticks. Such "arrangements" have become almost a hallmark of my work, but I did not invent "the single flower." The single blossom in its vase appears in works of art from the beginning of time.

And single flowers are not my only liking. I love the beauty of a garden in bloom transported inside the house. And arrangements that are totally inspired by the growth of flowers; or by a handful of flowers picked at random from a garden or a meadow.

I am often asked, "Where did you learn?" I was never

An extraordinary double-ruffled variety of lisianthus, white dotted with violet, combined with violet lisianthus in its more usual single form makes a lilting bouquet for a Victorian vase. This kind of arrangement can never be exactly duplicated. Its artistry depends on attentive observation of the movement of the flowers at hand and careful cutting and placement to take advantage of that movement. Photograph by Guy Lindsay.

taught to arrange flowers, but I have never stopped learning—and there is always so much more to see and to know. All of my knowledge comes from looking at and feeling Nature.

Look attentively at the way plants grow: Do they grow in graceful curves or stiff and straight? Do the blossoms normally face up toward the sky—iris—or out—sunflowers—or down toward the earth—several kinds of lilies? Are the blossoms spread along the top of downward-curving branches as they are in dogwood or euphorbia fulgens or freesia? Or clustered around the branch as in quince or cherry or forsythia? Or do they hang bell-like below the leaves as they do in fuchsia or wisteria? A flower's natural habits are the best guide you can have to placing it attractively in a container, whether your bouquet is made of just one kind or many different ones.

Nature is a wonderful teacher, but there are others. A great artist once said that it is not a beautiful sunset that inspires someone to become a painter, but a beautiful painting of a sunset. You can train your eye by looking carefully at arrangements you admire in museums, houses you visit, flower shops, magazines, books. Even when an arrangement is a simple bunch of flowers—a dozen tulips or three stalks of lilies—it will repay a thoughtful consideration of the proportion of flowers to container, the relation of the colors and textures of the flowers to the texture and color of the container. With designs made up of different kinds and colors of flowers there are more—and more complex—relationships to notice and appreciate.

Look at the way flowers are arranged in works of art, in Egyptian murals and bas reliefs, Roman and Byzantine mosaics, Medieval tapestries and altarpieces, Persian and Indian miniatures, Chinese and Japanese scrolls and screens and lacquerware, and

❧

One spray of 'Pink Glory' lilies, one white rose and a pair of galax leaves in a vase that is much less precious than it looks: Underneath the gold-leaf plating it is a simple glass container in the gourd shape beloved of Chinese potters. Photographs by Roger Bester.

❧

Variation on the theme: The container, tied with a cord to emphasize its derivation from a real gourd used as a flask, and the stand are very slightly different. Two stems of *Nerine sarniensis* make a bright orange posy in a ruff of galax leaves and aromatic oakmoss tied up with a raffia bow. Two more galax leaves at the mouth of the vase balance the composition and keep the nerines standing straight.

Backed by the pleats of a fan palm leaf, a pair of strelitzia blossoms really do look like birds of paradise. Moss-buffered raffia holds them back to back, more moss fills the mouth of the container to stabilize their heraldic symmetry. The often stiff shapes and large scale of tropical leaves and flowers seem to look particularly well treated with architectural formality. Ribbon trick: the wide moss-green moiré band around the top of the ceramic cylinder brings into harmony white container and green moss. Indeed, the long, curling ends of the simply knotted ribbon might be taken at first glance for another kind of tropical leaf.

❧

Flowers, both casually and carefully arranged, add their charm and fragrance to a sitting-room corner overlooked by the Douanier Rousseau's joyful vision of Eden and filled with choice objects and treasured photographs. A handful of lilies of the valley in a crystal jug shares a lamp table with Chinese and European porcelains. A little Henry Moore bronze on another table partners both an informal bunch of full-blown roses in a silver tumbler and a moss-covered topiary ball decorated with swags of pink and red dried rosebuds. Photograph by Mick Hales.

European paintings from the Renaissance to the present day. I'm in complete agreement with the distinguished flower arranger and historian Julia Berrall that "the study of masters of painting is immensely valuable. Their combinations of flowers may have been at times unnatural, but never their delineation of the flowers themselves. They were careful, always, to preserve the inherent qualities of line and form that each flower possesses."

Today, in fact, some of these "unnatural" combinations—spring, summer, and autumn flowers in a single bouquet—don't seem unnatural at all. Air freight has made available to us flowers from all the world's seasons at any given moment. Scientific understanding of the necessary blooming conditions for a great many flowers enables growers to manipulate light and dark, heat and cold, water and its withholding, and trick those flowers into blooming out of season in the greenhouse. As the painters knew, it is form and line, color and texture and size that really determine whether flowers look well together. If we prefer to stick to seasonal arrangements, and many people do, it is probably because they create the mood of a season, which may conjure up a cherished memory for us.

Composing with flowers is like making sculpture. But we are composing a work of art out of materials that are natural works of art, and we should respect them. Many kinds of flowers—carnations, cockscombs, marigolds, even roses, especially the awkward stiff-stemmed commercial ones—are particularly effective gathered edge to edge in a monochrome or multicolor bunch. It's the same principle as the mixed-flower Victorian nosegay. Lately however, there seems to be an unfortunate inclination to stuff so many flower heads together that they look smothered—"mashed"

rather than "massed." And I don't like using wires to force flowers into some position that they resist falling into on their own. If you do have to hold them in a particular position, there are ways to do it with natural materials like moss and leaves and bamboo and raffia that can be made part of the design.

In arranging flowers we have to bring into harmony three elements: the flowers themselves, the container, and the space that surrounds them.

The container is generally fixed in size and shape and color, but not always, as we shall see later on. To find which containers work best with the decoration of your house and with the places you like to put flowers, you simply have to experiment. You may enjoy building a varied collection of containers or prefer to limit yourself—or be limited by the space you have—to the minimum of sizes and shapes that you need. You may wish to choose your containers to enhance certain kinds of flowers that you love or you may choose instead flowers that look well in containers of which you are fond. The more suited flowers and container are to each other, the more beautiful each looks. I can't give a rule to follow. Any rule that would cover every situation would have so many qualifications that you could never remember it. You have to train and trust your own eyes and the best way to do that is to keep arranging flowers.

For single flowers or all-of-a-kind flowers, I particularly like clear glass because I can see the stems—and, as a practical matter, keep track of the level of water. I use a ring of leaves to buffer the flower from the cold of the glass. Flowers in nature usually come protected by leaves, and interpreting what I see and feel from nature is my prime concept in arranging flowers. For mixed bouquets or more complex arrangements I usually prefer opaque containers—a mixture of stems is not often pleasing. In this

In a complex balancing act, the stiff-bladed leaf of a fan palm displays its hard-edge symmetry behind an asymmetric swirl of eremurus, also known as foxtail lilies. A left-over section of palm stem tied across the top of the vase with raffia supports leaf and flowers—they are tied to it with more raffia—and sports unmatched raffia tassels. A strategically placed galax leaf and a tuft of Spanish moss finish off the design. Eremurus, which stands straight in the garden and when first cut, will take on curves if you snip off the tip and let at least half the blossoms on the flower spike open before you put it in an arrangement. Photograph courtesy of Gumps.

case I love abundance and seek to put into an arrangement the beauty of a garden in bloom.

The colors, textures, shapes, and sizes of the flowers you work with are the changeable, adjustable element. Changeable through choice, adjustable through cutting. Don't be afraid to cut. Just because the flower has a long stem when you start, it doesn't have to keep that stem. Nor should you feel that you have to use every flower you have gathered for your arrangement. If something just doesn't seem to fit in, set it aside. You can always put it in a vase of its own and find a spot for it. We need to step back and look at our composition every now and then as we work, and teach ourselves to know when to stop. It also helps to turn the arrangement around every so often or else walk around and look at it from every angle.

Space, the space a flower arrangement occupies, is another variable, subject to your point of view and, to a degree, to the size of your rooms. You can consistently make arrangements for certain spaces in the house. Many people, indeed, prefer to create their designs right on the spot where they will go. But you can also create your design and then find or make space for it.

Space as volume is not all we have to consider in composing designs for our houses. We have to be aware of the color of the wall or background, its pattern if it has one, the pattern and color of any objects or fabrics that will be next to it. Rarely do we have in our rooms any equivalent to the Japanese tokonoma—an unfurnished, neutrally colored space where a flower arrangement, accompanied or not by a complementary painting, can be contemplated without competition from any other decorative element in the room. Only in some very spare modern interiors do you find such a space. But we do not invest a flower arrangement with symbolic or religious meaning as the Japanese do, and do not think of it as being on the same level of artistic value as, say, a piece of sculpture or a painting. We are more likely, if we think about it at all, to rank a superb flower arrangement with such objets d'art as porcelains, bronze or wood figurines, lacquer and enamel boxes. More often we consider it simply one among many decorative elements in a room. But then, we also frame and group paintings as decoration. I don't feel that our arrangements are any less sensitive, any less works of art. They are just different, created for a different context but based on a similar knowledge of and respect for all the possibilities of the flowers, the branches, the leaves that are our materials.

And again I say that we learn about flowers by living with them and working with them. By doing and doing arrangements you will get better every time, and the doing will become more and more pleasurable.

A crescent of late autumn flowers overflows a nineteenth-century French vermeil wine cooler on an English Regency console of fruitwood-inlaid Cuban mahogany. An identical wine cooler plays a very different role. Set on an Empire plant stand it is host to a delicate dendrobium orchid. The mass of the flowers may be different but their curves are sympathetic, both to each other and to those in the furnishings of this living room decorated by James O'Brien in a contemporary interpretation of that early nineteenth-century style known as Empire in France and Italy, Regency in England, and Federal in the United States. The chair in the corner is Austrian and the pair of chairs flanking the console, Italian. The canterbury, the pedestal side table, and the embossed silvered leather screen are English, and the mirror American but late nineteenth century. Photographs by Guy Lindsay.

In the console arrangement, downward-curving branches of eucalyptus, bayberry, and hydrangea create the underlying form for a bountiful gathering of dahlias, roses, and lisianthus punctuated with apples, and bracketed by giant white Casa Blanca lilies at either end.

The perfect globe on a single stem is a great classic of topiary art: the boxed orange trees at Versailles are always shown so shaped in seventeenth- and eighteenth-century engravings. To grow a plant and train it by clipping and wiring takes careful attention and several years. Attention is also needed for faux topiary—leaves or flowers or fruit attached to a moss-stuffed frame or a plastic foam form—but the timetable is measured in minutes and you can create combinations undreamed of in nature. Here, "planted" in a silvered miniature Versailles box, a birch-branch stem bears a globe paved with champagne grapes, pale green hydrangea florets, and orange nerines. Painting by Fred Weymer. Photograph by Guy Lindsay.

Precious and similar but not identical objects and bouquets paired in a symmetrical arrangement on a marble-topped chest: Ormolu-mounted porphyry urns flanking a Louis XVI French marble and gilt bronze clock case are in turn flanked by vigorous Tang Dynasty horsemen. The bouquets seem to match, but if you study them closely you will see that the impression is created by a few flowers carefully placed—the two inward-curving Estella Rynveld parrot tulips, the two tall yellow eremurus, the white lilacs and Queen Anne's lace below them, and the white lilacs just above the mouth of the urn. Around them leaves and flowers—more parrot tulips, hybrid tea and 'Doris Rijkers' floribunda roses, ranunculus, and ixia—are allowed to follow their own bent, giving the arrangements a vitality that can be easily lost in the attempt to achieve rigid symmetry. Photograph by Mick Hales.

Happy meeting of East and West. The container, a bronze gourd, and its lacquer base are Japanese, as are the proportions of flowers to container. But the flowers themselves and the casual, windblown mood of the arrangement are very American. The blossoms are delicate: blue lace flowers, Iceland poppies, California poppies (*Eschscholzia*), rose buds, and a sweet sultan. Much of the lively movement emanates from the willful, twisting green buds of the lace flowers and poppies. Delicate stems in such an open arrangement must be anchored in some kind of holder. In this case it is chicken-wire mesh. Photographs courtesy of Gumps.

The same bronze gourd plays host to a much smaller and more compact bouquet of similar flowers: three golden California poppies and a bud, one rosy Iceland poppy and a bud, a rosebud that marries their colors plus two blue lace flowers, a few sprigs of poppy foliage, the perfectly arched stem of a lace flower bud, and the scroll of an unfurling fern. All seem to be growing naturally, as if a clump of mossy soil with its diverse inhabitants had simply been lifted from the garden to the container. In truth, the moss conceals wire mesh and each stem was carefully placed.

Simplicity has its own charms, particularly if the flower arrangement is created to become one element in a larger arrangement of art objects on a table top. The appeal of these three stems of Rothschild lilies in a Chinese porcelain flask is as much a matter of concord and contrast as it is of satisfying proportion. The gold-edged petals match the sang-de-boeuf glaze; their rippling flame-like forms counter its smooth contours. The pair of galax leaves and the raffia-tied moss interpose symbolic "earth to grow from" between flowers and container.

53

❧

A large-scale arrangement in the
manner of eighteenth-century
flower painters like Jean-Baptiste
Monnoyer or the van Huysum
family combines *Hydrangea
paniculata* 'Grandiflora' and heavily
budded sprays of eucalyptus with
soft orange and buff-colored
hybrid lilies in a silver-gilt wine
cooler, and demonstrates that
lavishness does not need the wide
variety of flowers that could never
bloom together which is
characteristic of those painters.
This particular combination of
materials belongs to late summer.
In late spring or early summer an
arrangement in the same style
for the same room might be made

up of white lilacs, dogwood, pink
and white peonies or apricot and
pale yellow lily-flowered tulips.
Later on a splendid effect could be
achieved with roses only, given
access to a variety of garden
roses—sprays of tiny single
blossoms, fat old-fashioned
centifolias, shapely hybrid teas,
and clustered floribundas.
Photographs by Guy Lindsay.

❧

The arrangement is one of a pair
designed to flank the fireplace and
bring to life for a festive evening a
pied-à-terre apartment decorated
by James O'Brien.

A luscious early summer arrangement that might have come straight from the brush of Henri Fantin-Latour, even to the antique Japanese basket. Lilacs, pinky mauve and lavender blue, are the foundation for the design and suggested its shape: a branch that naturally forked in new-moon form. Pink peonies plus a couple of red-streaked white blossoms from that old-fashioned favorite peony 'Festiva Maxima' provide counterpoint. Lilacs and peonies seem to be natural partners, their shapes, textures, and colors mutually enhancing, and their blooming periods contemporaneous. You can get lilacs out of season, but not peonies, although their season has been somewhat lengthened by new storage techniques. They remain truly seasonal, one of the few flowers that do. All the leaves have been removed from the stems, principally because they would interrupt the close color harmony; but their removal also prolongs the life of the blossoms. The only touch of green comes in the buds of the blue lace flowers (*Trachymene coerulea*, also called *Didiscus*) and the sweet sultans, respectively the delicate blue and pink grace notes in the composition. Photograph courtesy of Gumps.

A white porcelain swan laden with pink and white blossoms sports a rather peacocky tail of snapdragons. In its layers of swirling curves the asymmetric composition echoes the movement of the container. Clouds of Queen Anne's lace set off deep rose hybrid lilies, pale pink peonies, and bright pink hardy gladiolus. These last, with their graceful habit and attractively marked petals, are hardy to Zone 4 and do not have to be dug and replanted every year—left alone they will naturalize. They are still less known and less frequently planted than the larger, showier but stiffer and more demanding gladioli to which we are accustomed. Photograph courtesy of Gumps.

FLOWERS FOR THE TABLE

On a table for two for a fireside supper, a nosegay of plain and parrot tulips, peonies, and sweet peas fringed with galax leaves fills two semicircular brass frames holding glass tubes, direct descendants of the eighteenth-century posy holder. Carrying on the theme, single glass tubes, each in its own frame and each bearing a delicate stem of ixia and two galax leaves, march across the mantel in front of an early painting by the great Brazilian landscape architect and painter Roberto Burle Marx. Galax-wrapped votive candles light the table. Silver and tortoise boxes and the beturbanned, painted lead drummer-on-horseback are just for fun. Photograph by Guy Lindsay.

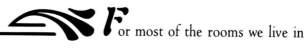

For most of the rooms we live in we can introduce the kind of flowers we like, arrange them to suit our own fancy, and place them wherever they please us. I really can think of only two exceptions, two places where the comfort and pleasure of others should play equally important roles in determining our materials and our designs. One is a shared bedroom, in which you would certainly accommodate your partner's allergies and aversions in your choice of flowers, in particular the highly scented ones. The other is the dining table. Whether you are setting your table for a simple family meal or a very special dinner, remember that the table decorations, floral or not, are just one element in the creation of an enjoyable social occasion. A centerpiece is not a monsterpiece; it should not block everyone's view.

What makes an appropriate centerpiece is not a matter of rules but of consideration. There are certain guidelines that I have found useful, but there have been situations in the past when it was justifiable to disregard them. Undoubtedly there will be others in the future. For an example, take the principle, which comes close to being a rule, that the centerpiece should not block the view across a table. I certainly prefer that flower arrangements on the dining table be well below eye level or else lifted a bit above it—I don't mind looking around a slender

Climbing, twining, cascading, feathery smilax so conceals the structure of a candelabrum that the white votive candles in their leaflike metal holders are apparent only on close inspection. Taller fat white candles might be more striking, but votive candles have a great advantage: They don't drip in a draft. Not that there is a draft in this dining room—the open arcades are a trompe-l'oeil mural by Michael Klaric. The smilax and the sprays of white dendrobium orchids are fixed in a container filled with water-retaining foam in the center of the specially designed candelabrum. A handsome ornament for the dining table between meals as well as a lovely way to keep candle flames above the eye level of diners, a design like this can be multiplied to make exceptionally effective table decorations for a large party. Flowers in any color and almost any shape can be substituted, and the candelabra can be spaced the length of a long table or, one to a table, center a collection of round ones. Photograph by Guy Lindsay.

shaft or pedestal and don't find that anyone else does either. Once, when I was doing flowers for a large charity dance, however, the committee specifically asked for really large table arrangements as the major decorative element for the party. They felt that it was impossible to talk to anyone on the other side of a round table large enough to seat ten people and therefore it didn't really matter whether or not you could see anyone on the other side of the table. There were no complaints about those centerpieces, but I still think that most people feel more comfortable with clear visibility.

You have more freedom when you are decorating a buffet table. Your arrangement need not be in the center of the table and it can be very large, in fact it should be. If the platters and chafing dishes don't leave enough room for a major decoration, it is really better to do without. Or to adapt the medieval idea of garlanding the platters with leaves and flowers. I very often use urns or other containers raised on a pedestal, which can support a quite large arrangement without occupying a lot of table space.

Allowing space for flowers is important—for me, as important as the space for the service of the table. But you don't invade the space that should be taken by the silverware and plates and glasses. Vines that twine around the stems of the glasses may look pretty in a photograph, but they are simply a nuisance at dinner. That doesn't mean that you shouldn't use your imagination. Far from it. By all means create a jungle on your table, but do tame the animals so that they don't bite your guests. What do I mean by that? Let's say you're making a mille fleurs tapestry garden for the center of the table. Aesthetically, it might be more effective to bring the sod right down to the edge of the table, but you would get everybody dirty. Your fantasy will be more admired if you keep the sod in its place—on a cookie sheet, perhaps—in the center.

Dinner for four with Meissen and a multitude of flowers. Tiny painted flowers ornament the rims of the Meissen porcelain dinner plates, giant embroidered flowers decorate the place mats and napkins, porcelain blossoms garland Meissen covered jars, and real blossoms cluster in a flowery Meissen bowl. Only the porcelain-handled knives and forks and the eighteenth-century boxes eschew flower motifs in favor of more stylized patterns. In the background, a painting by the well-known nineteenth-century English painter of equestrian subjects A. J. Munnings hangs over a console displaying a cabbage tureen and two antique figurines. The centerpiece bouquet, seen from a different side in each of the three views shown, includes roses of several kinds and colors, ranunculus, poppies, lilies, sweet peas, freesia, grape hyacinths, parrot tulip buds, and pale green viburnum corymbs. Photographs by Mick Hales.

You can always hide the edge by fencing your meadow with bamboo or twigs, which would be both attractive and historically accurate.

One warning. When you're trying out a new idea for a party centerpiece, try it out for yourself first. The last-minute madness of attempting to bring off a complicated arrangement can ruin the evening for you and your guests alike. Usually, in fact, the flowers for a party are best if they are done the day before. This is what I like to do in my own home, not just because I will have more time the day of the party to attend to small details, but also because the flowers will have opened up and be at optimum attractiveness. If any last-minute corrections are necessary, I can make them easily. Unfortunately, it is not always possible to arrange everything ahead of time, in which case it is best to stick with a familiar arrangement, something you have done many times before.

Whether or not to use strongly perfumed flowers—hyacinths, narcissus, jasmine, gardenias—on the dining table is truly a question of personal taste. For some people they interfere with the enjoyment of the food and wine; for others they really enhance the experience of the meal. If you don't know your guests' sentiments on scent, it's wise to stay on the side of delicacy.

If practice makes flower arranging a pleasure, it is planning that perfects entertaining. Planning that ensures a relaxed host and hostess with all their attention given to welcoming their guests, secure in the knowledge that the decoration of room and table are as they wish, that drink and food will appear when wanted—or, if there is no help, with grace and ease on their part. With advance organization you can even enlist the aid of your guests and make it seem an enjoyable part of the evening; without

Summertime flowers in a summertime bowl for lunch on a city terrace or a suburban patio. The shell of a watermelon after the sweetest of its rosy flesh has been scooped out for dessert makes a stylish container for a great big bunch of daisies. The combination is particularly refreshing for a hot day, but daisies are by no means the only flower for a watermelon bowl. Consider baby carnations or zinnias, masses of white or multicolored phlox, or a drift of Queen Anne's lace, cascading petunias or nasturtiums. Photograph by Guy Lindsay.

careful organization it could become a disaster. One friend who lives in a small apartment without a separate dining room never hesitates to give dinners for fifteen or eighteen people. At just the right moment during cocktails she announces that it's time to set up the tables and divides the guests into teams, usually with someone on each who has been there before and knows the drill. One team fetches folding tables and chairs from the bedroom, and sets them up. Another puts on the tablecloths and napkins, also neatly stacked in the bedroom. Candlesticks and bowls of flowers that have been clustered on the hall table are retrieved and set in place; and a fourth team stashes cocktail glasses in the dishwasher, picks up trays of glasses, china, and silver from the kitchen and sets them out. While all this is taking place—and it doesn't take more than ten or fifteen minutes—the hostess does the final heating and finishing of the dinner and a gentleman guest, appointed to the task, uncorks the wines and puts them on the tables. It's a break that stirs up the party and guests always seem rather proud of having made a contribution.

For some strange reason, many people have the idea that planning inhibits spontaneity. The reverse is true. Planning makes spontaneity possible, at least in entertaining. Planning ensures that you always have the ingredients on hand to whip up a bowl of your special pasta for the six hungry teenagers your son brings home from the football game, or the couple you haven't seen in five years who turn up on an hour's notice, or the friends you're inspired to sweep home after the concert. Or, if cooking is really not one of your talents—and you live in a reasonably large town—that you have next to the telephone the numbers of at least three reliable sources of delicious delivered-to-the-door-in-a-half-hour meals.

Versailles boxes don't have to contain ball-and-stem topiaries. Miniature versions of the transportable planting boxes used in the gardens at Versailles for tender plants like oranges, lemons, and bay that had to be moved indoors during cold weather, they are equally hospitable to tight flower bouquets. Left, a white carnation hemisphere fills a metal-lined box of pale and tawny wood. Photograph by Roger Bester.

A silvered metal box holds a fragrant tussie-mussie of roses, nerines, narcissus, grape hyacinths, lavender freesia, and white viburnum. Such compact arrangements, portable and versatile, are a blessing to anyone who loves spur-of-the-moment hospitality. Move one to a terrace table for lunch, to the center of the dining table for dinner, take it back to its habitual spot in the living room or upstairs to a chest of drawers in the guest room: It adjusts to every change of scene with grace. Photograph by Peter Margonelli.

True, it is often not possible to fix up a flower arrangement for the table on really short notice. But is there an arrangement somewhere else in the house that could double as a centerpiece? Or two or three single flowers to nestle at the foot of a candelabrum? Or fruit that could be piled in a bowl or a basket? Or do you have in your closet a handsome tureen, a large and fascinating shell or a beautiful porcelain bowl that needs no additional embellishment to effectively decorate the center of the table? At night, in fact, all you really need are lots of candles to make a table festive.

Nighttime for me is the time to relax and enjoy friends and family. Only on weekends can I entertain at lunch, and this seems to be true for most of my friends and clients as well. When I do set a table for lunch, I like flowers that are light, full of movement. And at lunch—or breakfast for that matter—I like to use all the lovely

❦

Most adaptable arrangement, a
fragrant hemisphere of pink roses
and pink sweet peas, creamy roses
and white sweet peas, all laced
with white didiscus in a lacquered
canister. Such small mixed
bouquets in attractive containers
fit to perfection the centers of the
card-table-sized dining tables in
most small apartments, and they
can be multiplied to suit a larger
table, even set marching the length
of a banquet board. Photograph
by Marisa Alvarez Lima.

❦

Also of the accommodating kind,
a posy of pink roses, rosy freesia,
red godetia, lavender sweet peas,
and white Queen Anne's lace fills
an Indian silver goblet. A bouquet
like this is perhaps the best way to
bring flowers to your hostess, if
for some reason you must bring
them with you. Is there a
household that could not find a
place for such a one in an instant?
Still, it is always easier for the
hostess if guests send flowers well
ahead of the party or the following
day as a thank-you. Photograph by
Marisa Alvarez Lima.

blue flowers that wash out under artificial light. Very often I simply put a single blossom in its vase in front of each guest. In the evening arrangements can, even should, be more elaborate.

On my dining table I usually set a votive candle at each place because it throws a very flattering light on the face. A low light on the table brings all the features of the face up. When you have candles at the height of your eyes the flickering of the flames can be very distracting and annoying. Candles should either be raised well over the eye level or set very low.

And the light around the table, the ambient light, is important. I do not believe in

❧

Set for lunch another day, the table gets a different centerpiece— a low arrangement of bright blue cornflowers and delicate pink hydrangeas with their own leaves in a Japanese "majolica" box— but the appointments do not change. And they are a lesson in the liveliness that unmatched elements can bring to a table setting as long as they have some sort of relationship. Here, for example, the salt cellars and pepper shakers, though approximately the same size, are different at each place; the bread and butter plates and place plates don't match but both patterns are of Oriental inspiration; the knives and forks have related but not identical designs; and each of the silver boxes is one of a kind. Photograph by Mick Hales.

spotlights over tables. Light from straight overhead drags your face down. The shadows created by your nose over your lips are a disaster. You cannot be in the dark with just the table illuminated; it would look as if you were in a spacecraft. You need light all the way around you, but very soft light reflected from walls and ceiling.

A combination of chandelier and wall sconces is the classic way to achieve even lighting in a dining room. If these fixtures are electric ones, do have dimmers for them. Then you really can control the light level. Another solution is to use uplights in one or two corners of the room, a particularly pleasing one when they shine up through the leaves of plants and cast shadows across the ceiling. And don't forget candles. Wherever you can find space for them—on mantels, sideboards, consoles, side tables, windowsills—they will create a warm and flattering glow.

If you have set your table outdoors on a terrace, one of the most attractive ways to create a magic circle of light is to place not-too-strong floodlights at the base of two or three trees and aim them to illuminate the canopy of leaves. I like best for this purpose light that is cool, almost bluish, like moonlight. Colored lights, including green which always looks artificial, are fine for a big party when they are part of a whole fantasy; but they call too much attention to themselves for a relaxed dinner party.

It always seems to me that table flowers for outdoor meals, day or night, should be similar to those that grow in the garden or in the fields beyond. Familiar, not exotic. But exotic is a very relative adjective. The garden roses or petunias, daisies or Queen Anne's lace or black-eyed Susans that seem so simple and natural in our northern summers would seem as exotic in Florida or Hawaii or Southern California as their plumbagos or plumerias, anthuriums or hibiscus, or fragrant gingers seem to us.

Sophisticated color shadings, a rich play of textures, and an unusual combination of materials characterize a bouquet for a buffet table. Orange lilies, red-orange nerines, soft pink sedum, strong pink roses and panicles of pale green hydrangea spring from a cushion of deeply ruffled blue-green kale. Foliage vegetables—lettuce, cabbage, watercress, mustard, chard as well as kale—and vegetable foliage—beet greens, carrot tops, squash and grape vines—are easy to come by and, well conditioned, valuable resources for the flower arranger. Photograph by Guy Lindsay.

A bouquet of vegetable flowers, cauliflower and broccoli, which we pick to eat—or arrange—in the bud, gets a ruff of galax leaves and a seasoning of pink roses. The container is wrapped in cinnabar moiré to echo the outlines of the low lacquer table. Photograph by Marisa Alvarez Lima.

A patch of jungle transported to a table set for a buffet. The high canopy is a phoenix palm, the understory a very untropical but attractive mix of delphiniums, double tulips, anemones, roses, and clivia each in its own bud vase. The bowl of fruit remains part of the table decoration until the end of the meal, when it offers one of several dessert choices.

Photograph by Roger Bester.

❦

Welcome times five at a lunch for four. A quincunx of miniature pineapples, each in its own Indian silver vase, fills the center of a Danish Victorian inlaid fruitwood dining table ringed with English Regency chairs. Between meals, or simply for a change of pace, the pineapples can be dispersed to enliven shelves or side tables in this apartment living room designed by James O'Brien. Photograph by Guy Lindsay.

❦

At dinnertime in the same city living room, the silk organza undercurtains are drawn, the table appointments are more elaborately decorated, and the centerpiece is a mosaic of color. The tightly set and totally non-seasonal bouquet gathered in the Indian repoussé silver vase includes dahlias, amaryllis, ranunculus, and parrot tulip buds—a testament to the horticultural and marketing prowess of modern flower growers. Votive candles in gold-plated glasses shaped like miniature flowerpots provide the light. Photograph by Guy Lindsay.

❧

An overscaled arrangement for the entrance hall of a formal town house is designed to draw guests up to a second-floor living room. Tremendous lengths of bamboo fan out from a fabric-wrapped tub; cords of many colors loop through the bamboo; orchids of many kinds and colors dangle from the cords or spray up from moss at the end of some bamboo stalks. The whole composition demands a large space: There is nothing shy about the hall table and the waterlily-print chintz that covers it—a square cloth tied tightly at the corners over a matching gathered skirt. The double-gourd-shaped glass vases holding lilies and a peony on the table are the same as those holding orchids that, yoked together with bamboo rods, sway from the cords. Photograph by Roger Bester.

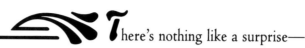

There's nothing like a surprise—a happy surprise, to be sure—to start a party off on the path of gaiety which is the whole point of parties. The surprise can, of course, be the music, or a special entertainment, but what everyone sees first are the decorations. And they can be as exotic, as exciting, as evocative of distant times and places—or an imagined future—as you wish to make them. Stimulation not relaxation is the goal, and a big party offers a chance to set your fancy free. There are limitations—about which more later—but they are not limitations of the imagination. Still, the imagination often needs a starter.

The occasion for the party may be a source of inspiration. Paper, china, silver, golden anniversaries all suggest decorative points of departure. Perhaps there is something in the career of the person in whose honor the party is given: a soprano particularly famous for her *Traviata* or *Butterfly*, a businessman who is also a ski fanatic, a writer who is known for his interest in the Turkish Empire. The interpretation need be neither obvious nor elaborate. In the last-named case, for example, you might center the tables with bouquets of red lily-flowered tulips and base your color scheme on the blue, green, lacquer red, and white of Isnik pottery.

When you are fortunate enough to have a space with good

☙

Spaces of heroic size like the two usually used for gala entertaining at The Metropolitan Museum of Art in New York—the Blumenthal Patio and the Temple of Dendur—demand decorations on a heroic scale. Not all museums have rooms of quite this size or architectural distinction, but in most the rooms are well designed, and in almost every room where museum parties are given, at least some beautiful objects from the collection are present. Such rooms demand a dignified scheme that respects the art and the architecture as well as bringing warmth and festivity to the occasion. All photographs by Eric Weiss.

proportions and strong architectural character you can follow the lead of the location for the theme, the mood, even the flowers. Paintings, tapestries, porcelain and pottery of the period will give you more than enough examples of the kind of garlands and bouquets that will enhance a room paneled in the Louis XV style. The *boiseries* themselves may even provide models to enlarge and bring to life and color with flowers. But you don't have to stick to the roses of that rose-possessed age. What's important is that the flowers be familiar denizens of the temperate garden and be loosely and informally arranged. Moderne and Art Deco interiors, on the other hand, cry out for the bold shapes and glossy textures of tropical leaves and blossoms in highly stylized arrangements, symmetrical or asymmetrical.

Today the great majority of big parties are given to benefit charities, and even the most architecturally interesting country clubs, hotel ballrooms, and museum halls seem to need an extra dose of fantasy when they are the setting year after year for the same charity dinner-dance. More often, alas, the designer, professional or volunteer, has to deal not just with the same space every year but one that is undistinguished if not downright ugly. Total transformation usually costs more than the budget allows, so the challenge is to shift the guests' attention away from the room and focus it on the table decorations or on a few spectacular and well-lit areas. If the room is large you may have to depend on fabric, or lattice panels, or trees, or balloons to create the principal effect and use flowers simply as accents. The more accustomed you become to looking at any and every material for its decorative potential, the better fueled for the challenge your imagination will be.

There is a danger. Don't try to use every idea you have, every material you think

Great garlands of sprengeri
embroidered with rubrum lilies
and sprays of white dendrobium
orchids, as well as streamers of
Spanish moss cascade from the
railing of the Cantinori or singing
balcony on one side of the
Blumenthal Patio. The Patio was
created from fragments of
sixteenth-century architecture in
carved marble, principally from
Spain but also from Italy.
Garlands are right at home
here—Priapus and Flora, the
statues by Bernini that guard the
doorway, wear, respectively,
garlands of fruit and of flowers on
their heads. Bernini's bacchic *Faun
Teased by Cupids* in the foreground
is a permanent inhabitant, but a
fortuitously appropriate one for
the site of the cocktail hour.

The principal garlands, about fifteen feet long and built on wire frames, are supplemented at the sides of the balcony by hanging baskets of sprengeri, ornamented with the same mix of flowers.

has possibilities for the same party. In photographs, I've seen decorations combining balloons and feathers and flowers that I find a disaster. When you try to do too much, you *do* too much. I would not go quite as far as Mies van der Rohe's "Young man, mix martinis not materials," but I do find that too many materials of different kinds create confusion instead of drama.

Decorating for big parties is truly a question of proportions. When you are dealing with high ceilings you can have height in your decorations. If you are dealing with a low ceiling and try to do something too high or too large, people will feel suffocated and the ceiling seem even lower. Truly large-scale arrangements are for large-scale spaces.

What I like to do is keep the flowers at the eye level of someone standing up, particularly when people will be standing and having drinks in a room that looks into the dining room. If you keep the flowers at that height you have a feeling you are looking into a garden. If I have a space with very high ceilings and I decide to do low flowers on the tables, I surround the tables with something—perhaps palm trees or bamboos full of orchids—that will create height and compensate for the low flowers.

Lighting is very important. Very often public spaces—hotels, museums—are much too bright. You want to turn the lights down so the room becomes more romantic, cozier, and the best way is to use dimmers if you possibly can. You can use spotlights to direct attention to arrangements at the sides or ends of a room, but pinspots over the tables are extremely difficult, almost dangerous, to handle. The spot must be exactly over the top of the centerpiece arrangement and precisely focused. If there is any angle to the beam it may hit someone in the face and it is blinding. It can be fantastic for the flowers and wreck the guests. Essentially, lighting the tables for a large party is the same as lighting your own dining table—there are just more tables to light. And, as at home, you need to create a soft, even ambience in the room and balance the light so that no one area is either too bright or too dark.

Over and over I keep coming back to the painter Ingres's advice that one must always work with the ensemble in mind—the whole space, the light and shadow, the total effect. Do not concentrate on some small part without bearing the whole in mind.

If planning helps produce a relaxed and charming dinner for a few friends, it is absolutely crucial for a large party. Ideally, you should start about four months ahead. You don't need to get neurotic and spend a year planning, but don't leave things to the last moment. Any occasion that demands the sending of invitations has to have lead time for the printing and the mailing. Today, with the Post Office the way it is, allow six weeks to send invitations and receive answers. Otherwise you have to start preparing the party before you get all the answers back, and you really need to have your guest list established a month ahead. Every caterer will have five to ten extra serving portions to allow for last-minute additions—but never more than that.

Another thing that is very important is the time schedule. When will the room be available to decorate? When will the caterer come to set the tables? When will the music start to play? When will guests start to arrive? When will the musicians take a break? When will all the different events—speeches, presentations, special entertainment—happen during the course of the event? Set up a schedule and give it to everyone who is working on the party. Or engage the services of a good party coordinator and then leave it to him or to her to do all the scheduling.

Two-story arcades fill two walls of the Blumenthal Patio. On the side facing the balcony, a big bouquet of sprengeri, lilies, and orchids clasps the base of each column on the second story. The sixteenth-century marble Orpheus contributes a permanent note of celebration.

Enormous bouquets in terra-cotta
pots on metal stands decorate the
other second-story gallery. The
flowers are mostly white—Shasta
daisies, lilies, and lilacs—with a
dash of deep pink contributed by
the rubrum lilies.

Guests entering the glass-walled home of the Temple of Dendur for dinner and dancing are greeted by what seem the flames of a thousand candles. Votive lights clustered on floating metal lily pads are reflected in the water of the pool that surrounds the temple platform and re-reflected in the sloping glass walls. Inspiration came from the giant leaves of the water lily *Victoria amazonica*, also known as *Victoria regia*, which will support a small human being, but the idea would have pleased the lotus-loving Egyptians.

❧

In such enormous space decorations should be concentrated at a limited number of strategic points. Additional palm trees supplement the pair that flank the rear of the Temple. Lights and flowers gleam on the tables arrayed on the lower platform, one step down from the platform that holds the two parts of the temple.

❧

In the center of each table a flat basket holds a compact but informal cluster of scented blossoms—white lilies and lilacs accented with purple freesia and blue grape hyacinths—tucked between galax leaves and set in florist's foam.

The tables are skirted to the floor with glossy bronze-colored moiré, and the glass table appointments, plates as well as wine and water glasses, add sparkling reflections to the light from the ring of galax-wrapped votive candles that surround the centerpiece.

Giant bouquets in boxes mark the change in level on both sides. Two dripping sprengeri and orchids soften the granite wall that surrounds the platforms. Many of the flowers used in the Blumenthal Patio bouquets are repeated in the big box bouquets, but with a different mood, Egyptian in feeling although not re-creating recorded Egyptian arrangements. Long stems of speciosum lilies, white and pink, tied to tall, flexible bamboo canes for support, provide the needed height. Joining them are quince branches, white lilacs, Shasta daisies, and palmetto leaves, some adorned with sprays of orchids. Any water pick needed for a high-flying flower is camouflaged with a bit of Spanish moss.

You should not have to worry about anything that's happening once you begin to greet your guests. If you have not hired a party coordinator and are entertaining in a restaurant, make the maitre d'hotel responsible for seeing that everything happens on schedule and all emergencies are handled promptly. In a hotel, there is always one person you can put in charge so that no one ever has to come to you. If a wheelchair is needed, or a doctor, or someone to put a button on a blouse, or to deal with wine that's spilled on a guest, it should be taken care of by the person in charge of the party. The party should roll well and the host and hostess should not be concerned about anything else.

Delegating responsibility is just as important when you have to depend on volunteers rather than professionals to put on your party, but it works a little differently. It is usually a good idea for the whole group or committee to discuss and decide on the theme and the kind of decorations and menu they want. But once the basic decisions are made, the chairman should make up a schedule and give each person or committee a clearly defined task to perform, a realistic budget, an accurate deadline, and complete responsibility for its performance. If the whole group tries to settle all the details, you will have endless discussion and no action. I can remember an occasion where it took a dozen discussing volunteers an entire day to set up a room that at other times has been set up for exactly the same kind of reception in two hours by a three-man professional team.

I often find myself in a situation where I'm the party coordinator and the decorator and the florist—three different jobs all in one. In that case I really need to know everything about the party. I need to know from the hosts and the caterer what the

A large dance floor with tables all
around it is like a hole in the party
when everyone is eating dinner
and no one is dancing. This
imposing pillar of flowers right in
the center was designed to give the
dance floor a focus and ended up
creating a kind of promenade in
the center of the ballroom which
invited guests to move around
before dinner and between courses
even when the band was not
playing. The arrangement is built
on a huge tree-trunk set in a
bucket of cement. Flowering
branches are nailed to the top, and
all the flowers, gerberas and lilies
in many different colors, are in
individual vials. Sprengeri flowing
down the trunk covers up all the
mechanics. Clusters of eucalyptus
leaves contribute a refreshing
scent and streamers of Spanish
moss, a touch of romance.
Photograph by Marisa Alvarez
Lima.

All the decorations for this dinner party for thirty people in a New York City apartment are based on the permanent decoration of the dining room. However, the furniture that usually occupies the room—dining table, chairs, one console, and a waterfont—was moved out for the evening so that all the guests could be in the same room. The host and hostess do not like dividing a party between two rooms, and prefer to give two dinners on successive nights if they want to entertain more friends than the dining room will hold. The same chintz that upholsters the walls and curtains the windows of the dining room covers the round tables. The little gilt ballroom chairs pick up the gleam in the gilt frames of the mirrors and appliqués. With so many chairs and tables, space for flowers was limited to the mantelpiece, a console across the room, and the table centers.

The centerpieces and console bouquet are identical: compact compositions of grapes, galax leaves, and roses in very classic gilt-wire English baskets. Placing the bunches of grapes is the first step in such an arrangement. Their stems are wired to wooden picks and inserted in the block of florist's foam that fills the dark green basket-liners. Then the roses and the galax leaves are tucked in to complete the design. Particularly effective with the rich red of the dining-room chintz is the Fire and Ice rose, with its bi-color petals, crimson on the inside, white on the outside.

Garlands of sprengeri fringe a central mound of grapes and roses shading from palest pink through crimson, then trail across the mantel and down the sides of the chimney breast. Although this particular party took place in the early autumn, the colors, the flowers, and the touches of gold would be very effective in the holiday season. Photographs by Peter Margonelli.

Although it is an inside space, this private-party room in the distinguished New York restaurant Le Cirque has a light, open feeling because the tall arched mirrors act almost like windows. Not much was needed in the way of decoration to create a festive atmosphere for a private dinner party. But even when a room is less attractive than this, it is easier and more effective to concentrate on the tables, on the flowers and the tablecloths, and to treat the background in the simplest possible way. The choice of tablecloth can make a big difference. Most hotels and restaurants tend to use white, pale gray, or pale beige table linens, because they think those no-colors make the food look richer, and also, one suspects, because they are easier to launder. By bringing in a warm color for the tablecloths you make the room seem warmer and cozier, less impersonal. Photographs by Jade Albert.

Salmon pink cotton moiré tablecloths and napkins blend with the geranium pink of the restaurant's chair seats and reflect flattering tones on diners' faces. Ficus trees, one in each corner, are multiplied by the mirrors into a grove, and garlands on the wall help soften the background and bring a three-dimensional quality to it.

Centerpieces make the most of the sinuous curves that Iceland poppies fall into without provocation. Quartets of galax-ruffed flasks holding poppies are set in straight-sided glass bowls filled with water and polished black pebbles that gleam like dark mirrors.

food will be and how it will be served, and not just at the lunch or dinner, but before the meal as well. Because it does make a difference. If I'm going to have a big ice sculpture full of oysters, I will have to provide something so that the water will not be running everywhere. I need to take that into consideration in designing the decorations. Or choosing the color for the buffet tablecloth. If, let us say, platters of different meats are the main feature of the buffet and I use a very dark color on the table, the meat will look boring and unappetizing. I need to pick a color that will set it off. The more the person helping with the party knows about the party, the better it is.

Lately at large parties there is a tendency to put small gifts in front of each guest. This can become an annoyance, because there really isn't any place on the table for them. Tying up the napkins with flowers or napkin rings or small gadgets results in the same problem. Sometimes women can put them in their handbags, but men will never put them in their pockets. They end up on the chairs, eventually on the floor. It's much nicer if you give people their gifts on the way out, or, if you can afford the luxury, send them by messenger to guests' houses.

The garlands are simply attached to the lighting fixtures. Swagging or hanging garlands on the lighting fixtures has proved to be one of the best methods for decorating private party rooms in hotels, clubs, or restaurants for small or middle-size parties. It puts flowers at the eye level of standing guests in a manner that does not damage either the walls or the fixtures, and the garlands can all be made up ahead of time and installed in minutes. The foliage here is *Asparagus sprengeri*, usually called sprengeri fern or just sprengeri, sprinkled with pink roses, parrot tulips, orange lilies and, for zest, chartreuse cymbidium orchids. Sprengeri is particularly valuable because it makes a delicate-looking but strong foundation that can support water picks for all the flowers.

The little presents are a minor irritation, but I bring it up because no matter how beautiful the decorations, how magical the fantasy, people do not enjoy themselves at a party unless they are comfortable.

When you are working out the details of the table setting, be sure to take into consideration the diameter of the table (most tables for big parties are round today). If people are too far apart it makes conversation difficult, but a table that's too full takes away your freedom of movement. You need at least twenty-two inches of space between elbows for people to be able to eat comfortably. And things like salt and pepper should not be too far away. If you're going to have salt and pepper on the table, you should have a pair of shakers for every two people.

Be aware of steps, and be sure you make party guests aware of them too. In the daytime you can use plants or tall bouquets or ribbons—anything placed to draw attention to the change in level. Very often it is the single step that causes the most trouble. At night, see that steps are well lighted. In fact, you should illuminate well any area that can be dangerous.

A level surface is especially important when the setting for your party is a tent. If you have on your grounds a level space that is large enough—and be sure you measure it accurately—you can avoid the considerable expense of installing a floor and steps as well as a tent. You can still have a dance floor: it only takes up a small part of the surface and is not complicated to install. Whatever the circumstances, I have found that it pays to find people with good references who are experienced at setting up tents and to get bids from at least two different ones. If you are setting up the tent on the grounds of a museum or a country club or some other kind of public place, you

Making a grand entrance, sturdy lengths of bamboo, the upright ones set fast in boxes planted with orchids and *Monstera deliciosa*, are lashed together to create a monumental frame for a marble fountain in a marble niche. Spanish moss, asparagus ferns, and oncidium orchids drip from the dried grape vines that spiral up the niche and around the bamboo. Finishing touch for this fantasy grotto, tasseled silken cords suspend a pair of basket platforms for gerberas and lilies in crystal flasks. Photograph by Roger Bester.

An ornament of many uses, this urn bearing a ball of boxwood and set on a pedestal might have come from the garden of Sleeping Beauty's palace. A thick coating of moss and lichens covers urn and pedestal, a bird has built her nest in the box bush, and the lichens have climbed up to make a swag on it. You might even think the flowers had sprouted from airborne seeds were they not pink and white azalea clusters, which would have almost impossible difficulty growing up through a box bush. The underpinnings of this romantic construction are a wooden pedestal, a terra-cotta urn, and a chicken-wire ball filled with damp sphagnum moss. Sheets of moss are glued to urn and pedestal, lichens are tacked or glued, box and azalea twigs inserted in the sphagnum moss. It stands a bit over six feet tall and was created to stand at the foot of a staircase. Photograph by Joseph Mehling.

probably do not have to concern yourself with how and where your guests' cars will be parked. If the party is in your own house or garden you do. Your country club will know people you can hire who are well-trained to park cars. Or call the local police. They usually know people, and in many places handling party parking is a welcome source of additional income for off-duty policemen.

Also, few private houses have enough bathrooms for several hundred guests. For parties in tents you can get the kind of portable toilets used for construction sites. You can put them in a separate small tent or cover them with lattice panels or drape them to make them unobtrusive, and you have saved your guests from a lot of discomfort. It is very helpful to have an attendant in the ladies' bathrooms. You also should have soap and towels, needles and thread, but you don't need to go to the extreme of supplying lipstick and makeup—spot remover is much more useful.

There are a lot of wonderful ways to decorate a tent. The height, which is necessary for structural and ventilating reasons, immediately prompts taller decorations. I often use trees and branches, and I sometimes find myself tenting the tent with fabric to lower the ceiling so it doesn't seem impersonal, like a circus tent. Or you can just drape or swag fabric around the sides. You can create hedges and topiary to divide the space into separate areas for a receiving line if there is to be one, and for cocktails, dining, and dancing. Sometimes I break the rule of having a separate cocktail hour, thus avoiding the need for two tents. I put cocktails and dinner together, and it works perfectly. You have some trays passing and the buffet already open.

If you have a buffet service, the reason you have it is to encourage people to circulate. If you want people to circulate, you need to have space for them to walk.

You can't have as many places to sit as you have guests. If you have 200 guests you should have enough tables to seat 150 to 170. The seating areas should have a more informal air than they would for a seated and served meal—smaller tables with more chairs around and room for guests to walk among them. But don't serve food that must be cut with a knife.

Placing the buffet table in the center of the room or the tent helps circulation and is wonderful for the mood of the party. Everybody goes to the center of the room instead of clustering around one side or one end. As you get your plate and something to eat you start talking to someone. Maybe you all go to a table together and talk for a while. Then for the next course or dessert or coffee you can move to join other friends at different tables.

If for reasons of service the buffet must be at the end or one side of the party space, an important decoration in the center of the room will help to encourage circulation. For some reason people often seem reluctant to walk across a dance floor between sets, even to speak with friends. I have found that a column of flowers, or a large and elaborately decorated chandelier in the center will encourage them to move around when the orchestra is silent, turning the dance floor into a promenade.

Most of the party decorations for
this large diplomatic reception
were concentrated in the glass-
roofed patio just inside the House
of the Americas, the home of the
Organization of American States.
Oncidium orchids by the armload
and garlands of sprengeri and
Spanish moss were chosen to keep
the decorations in the same feeling
as the tropical plants and trees in
this indoor garden room.

The fountain in the center of the patio was assembled from pre-Columbian pieces and modern elements with similar motifs to look like an ancient fountain. The decorations imitate just what would happen naturally: Mosses and orchids would grow all over the stone in the tropics. Orchid-studded garlands of moss and sprengeri also cascade from the second-floor gallery and more orchids are sent climbing up the trunks of the palm trees that flank the front door.

For the buffet tables tall moss-covered chicken-wire cones are decorated with oncidium orchids and fruit—oranges, bananas, grapes, and pineapples, topped with a pineapple at the pinnacle. Tufts of gray Spanish moss disguise the water picks sustaining the orchids; the fruit is wired to the cone. Carrying on the theme, an orchid-spouting pineapple, not shown, occupies the center of each round dining table. Photographs by Marisa Alvarez Lima.

❦

Garlands of green ferns tied with
white satin bows on either side
of the door welcome wedding
guests to a stone church in an
Adirondack forest clearing. All
photographs by Peter Margonelli.

Few fashionable ladies in the
nineteenth century would have considered going to a party
without a bouquet to carry or perhaps a posy to pin to the
decolletage. That attractive custom, alas, has declined gradual-
ly to the point where the woman who even thinks of wearing or
carrying fresh flowers in the evening is quite rare, and the one
who does usually just wants a flower for her hair. Only for
weddings today do we almost automatically turn to flowers for
personal adornment as well as background decoration. Flowers
always seem to me a natural way to celebrate the ceremony of
marriage, and I always suggest that the bride carry a bouquet,
even if she has been married before, even if she is being married
by a justice of the peace. The bouquet can be simple, just a
handful of lilies of the valley or a dozen rosebuds. In fact, even
for the most elaborate formal wedding the bride's bouquet
shouldn't be too big. I've seen too many brides dwarfed by
bouquets that look like windowboxes. It's a matter of proportion. Only a very tall young woman can really carry off a cascade of flowers.

Try to follow nature, don't try to bend nature to your
wishes when you select your wedding flowers. That fantastic
divine white lily that you'd love to wear in your hair is going to
wilt in one hour, if it lasts that long. A headdress of fresh

❦

The bride's attendants hold nosegays of pink roses, pale for the maid-of-honor, deeper for the bridesmaids.

flowers or even one flower is a lovely idea. And wearing a wreath or crown of flowers is one of the prettiest and oldest traditions, one that goes back to ancient Egypt and appears in cultures all over the world. But you should pick a flower or flowers that will stay fresh and pretty for a long time; your florist can help you choose. The same holds true for your bouquet and those of your bridesmaids. Even we florists must be very careful with that bridal favorite, lily of the valley, and keep it in water right up to the time we give it to the bride so that it will stay fresh and strong. The unusual can be beautiful, but I would hazard a guess that a flower that has to come from Timbuctoo would only survive for a wedding in Timbuctoo. And lovely as it would be to carry wild flowers from the surrounding fields or forests for a rustic wedding, it is not always possible. Many wildflowers hang their heads the minute you cut them and quietly shrink away, refusing all attempts to revive them. Those that will survive need to be carefully conditioned and you will have to make time and space for this in your wedding preparations. If you know the effect you want it may be easier to achieve it with sturdier flowers from the garden or the florist.

Nature has plenty of durable flowers to choose from, and your choice is not limited to flowers. Your wedding bouquet is no longer expected to drive away witches and devils, and you would not be likely to compose it of powerful and powerfully scented herbs like garlic; but the rosemary and bay that were also carried at Medieval and Renaissance weddings might be ingredients in a charming and refreshing nosegay of sweet and spicy herbs for a wedding all in green and white. Or consider a sheaf of wheat, traditionally symbolic of fruitfulness in many cultures.

Because the wedding ceremony has such public as well as private importance, a whole series of customs, legal and religious requirements, and traditions sacred and

The bride carries a bouquet of
white freesia and lilies of the valley
in a frill of galax leaves.

secular have grown up around it. These very often differ from country to country and place to place within the same country. Who sends the invitations? How are they worded? How many attendants should you have and who should they be? Who pays for what? Who stands where? Don't feel that this is knowledge you should have at your fingertips; in today's small families marriages don't take place that often. Your florist may be able to help with some answers, but it is much better to consult a good up-to-date etiquette book or one of the books devoted especially to wedding etiquette or wedding planning. And ask the advice of your clergyman: there may be local variations or preferences that should be taken into account, and he can enrich the experience for you by explaining the symbolism of different parts of the ceremony.

A couple of generations ago it was the family of the bride who made most of the decisions and arrangements, and the time, place, and organization of the ceremony and reception were almost totally determined by tradition and community custom. All that has changed, perhaps too much; many traditions are beautiful and should not be discarded. But more about that later. Ever since the sixties, when brides and grooms might decide to be married on mountain tops and to write their own services, the wedding couple has had the decisive voice in the mood of the ceremony, even in cases where most of the detailed arrangements are made by the parents.

"Make up your mind, don't wait until the last moment," is my first piece of advice to any bride planning more than the smallest, simplest wedding. Your wedding day is your day to be a star, your chance to own the limelight. You need to decide what kind of production you want. Will it be formal or informal? Large or small? Follow closely the traditions of your religion or give individual expression to your and your bride-groom's beliefs? In a way, planning a wedding is like preparing a meal—first you

White gerbera and sprays of white dendrobium orchids backed by fluffy falls of asparagus fern hang from invisible wires looped over the pine-tree sconces flanking the communion table and spaced along the side walls of this Adirondack church.

Similar but simpler garlands are tied with white ribbons around every other pew. White lilies and white gerbera rise from beds of Boston ferns at the bases of the wrought-iron candlestands.

Green ferns and white flowers also compose the decorations inside. They are not the native ferns and white witch-hobble viburnum of the surrounding forest, but ingredients brought from New York City to create a similar atmosphere, since neither time nor facilities for conditioning wildlings were available on the spot. In fact, all the wedding bouquets and decorations were designed in the city, seven hours distant by car, on the basis of photographs and swatches supplied by the bride's family.

The reception took place in a rustic inn on a nearby lake, with cocktails on the veranda.

Two big bouquets of lilies and peonies in moss-covered jars on a table in one corner and, not shown, on the mantelpiece complete the decoration of the inn dining room.

❧ For the wedding supper, the most important piece of scene setting was the removal of printed curtains and placemats and their replacement with curtains and tablecloths of a soft beige sateen to blend with the polished board-and-batten pine walls. Each table is centered by a compact bouquet and lighted with galax-wrapped votive lights, including the five pushed together to make a T-shaped table for the wedding party.

❧ Peonies, roses, lilies, freesia, and brodiaea in varying proportions of pink and violet make up the centerpiece bouquets. Folded in the napkin at each place is a plump bag of lavender, a mosquito-repelling favor appropriate to a wedding in the woods.

decide what you are going to have, then you assemble the ingredients, and then you do the cooking.

We professionals can help you use your imagination to create the mood you want, but we cannot choose for you the mood you want to create.

For many brides choosing a wedding dress helps focus the mood they want to establish. It is interesting that when brides automatically think white or off-white for their dresses, they are still following a custom that is in fact quite recent. According to historians, white dresses for weddings first came into fashion at the end of the eighteenth century, and only became the norm during the Victorian period. Wearing a veil, on the other hand, is a very ancient tradition which goes back at least to Roman times but has moved in and out of fashion over the centuries. Even more than color, certain kinds of fabrics seem to belong in a certain kind of atmosphere: satins and brocades, lamés and taffetas definitely suggest a city setting. Country weddings seem to call for the lighter-weight silks, cottons, and linens; there, even in winter too luxurious a fabric seems out of place.

If you are wise, you don't try to mix the seasons and do a summer wedding in December. I grant that you could get the flowers. Unfortunately, today we don't have any seasons in flowers—you can get almost all of them almost all year round. But keeping your decorations in the feeling of the season, using the colors and flowers of the particular time of year, always seems more attractive. Going with the season need not be limiting; each season offers plenty of choices. If you don't care for the brilliant reds and oranges and golds of autumn leaves and bittersweet, you might choose the soft mauves and pinks and lavenders of asters and Michaelmas daisies with the pale beige of wheat.

*B*ouquets for the bride and for her attendants are normally very similar in size and shape. But the colors are often different and many times the flowers as well. Traditionally, the bride's bouquet is white, although today many brides choose to carry colored flowers and still others decide on all-white or all-green-and-white bouquets for themselves and their bridesmaids alike. With only a couple of exceptions—which are explained—the bouquets here are constructed very simply, the stems of the flowers bound together with florist's green paper tape. For a mixture of flowers it may be wound right down to the tip of the stems; but if the stems are attractive and all alike, the taped area may only be wide enough to fit the palm of the hand. Photographs by Fernando Bengoechea.

Caught in a ring of galax leaves, a galaxy and streamers of tiny white dendrobium orchids. The trailing streamers are simply the natural flower canes and need only to be bound in with the leaves, but the individual blossoms with their very short stems must be attached to longer tape-wrapped wire "stems" before they can be gathered into a bouquet.

❧

Long-stemmed lavender sweet peas are bound into a spray meant to lie gracefully along the arm. Here a few sprigs of wheat were tucked in among the flowers. Equally attractive would be sprigs of spring-green grass with sweet peas of any color; or the sweet peas might be replaced by feathery Michaelmas daisies, *Aster novae-belgii*, or New England asters in lavender or pink for an autumn wedding.

❧

A starry, sweet-scented cluster of stephanotis twined with ivy. Because its blossoms are virtually stemless—like camellias and gardenias, those other traditional bridal flowers—and must be wired to some kind of foundation, stephanotis lends itself to stylized arrangements. In this case wire is also used to hold the ivy in precisely placed curves.

❧

For the bride, a sheaf of curly, creamy white nerines in a galax collar; for the bridesmaids, the same bouquet might be duplicated in a choice of nerines—orange or pink or scarlet or red-and-white-striped. If white nerines are not to be found—they are much less common than their colorful sisters—a highly scented sub-stitute would be fully opened tuberoses.

Peonies and roses tightly bound in
a fluffy mosaic of pinks and reds
that range from palest shell
through apricot to carmine for a
bride who loves pink, either for
her own flowers or those of her
attendants. If she wants to carry a
white bouquet the same kinds of
flowers can be used. White
peonies with cream, white, and
shell pink roses would be a lovely
combination. When peonies are
out of season, a similar contrast of
textures can be obtained with
carnations.

Simple and simply lovely, a
handful of lilies of the valley with
their leaves in a collar of galax
leaves. Pale chartreuse-green
leaves like this come only on
forced, greenhouse-grown plants.
On lilies plucked from the garden
the leaves will be a darker green.
This is one flower that by custom
belongs to the bride alone, but to
give her attendants' bouquets the
same kind of simple delicacy they
might be composed of French-
Roman hyacinths or grape
hyacinths in either white or blue.

An open, informal mixed bouquet
of blossoms tucked among galax
leaves gathered into a circular
swirl includes roses, sweet peas,
lace flowers, pink and violet
lisianthus, a peony, a lily, white
freesia, white hyacinths, and a
sprig of white lilac. Such a design
is especially useful when you wish
to carry flowers from the garden
but do not have any one kind in
great variety, since it is hospitable
to blossoms of almost any shape or
color, alone or in combination.

❧

A pale pink rose centers concentric rings of pale lavender lace flowers, deeper pink roses, Queen Anne's lace, and galax leaves to form a tussie-mussie. Unlike the real Victorian tussie-mussies, however, this expresses no complicated message. The roses, indeed, stand for love; but neither lace flowers nor Queen Anne's lace seem to have found their way into the language of flowers. Such a tight, precisely arranged bouquet is best composed of round and rather flat blossoms or of very small ones, like violets, that can be clustered to help vary the texture.

❧

What could speak more clearly of a mid-summer wedding in the country than a handful of wheat and cornflowers tied with a raffia bow? Probably only a handful of wheat starred with one or both of the other two flowers that customarily grow in grain fields— daisies and scarlet poppies. But poppies, however appealing, present problems in a hand-held bouquet: they are very fragile and their stems exude a milky juice. The same effect is better achieved with red cosmos or godetia, both of which are easier to handle.

❧

Nestled among the roses and peonies in this nosegay are lavender sweet peas and white hyacinths for fragrance, and a single 'Stargazer' lily for drama. The same flowers in white would make a more subtle but equally interesting combination, since each one would display a different shade and texture of white.

For some brides the place where the wedding will be held is the most meaningful choice and the one that determines the mood, the decorative approach, and even the dress. Even if the location does not have a strong architectural or decorative personality, the broader distinctions between city and country, church or hotel or country club, house or garden, can't help influencing the mood. In addition, each different kind of location makes its own special demands on the design of the decorations.

In a church, the altar provides a built-in focus for the ceremony, and you may need or wish no more than special arrangements for the altar and small sprays of flowers or garlands or bows to decorate the pews along the aisle. How much more elaborate you wish to be depends on your budget—many families prefer to allocate more to decorating the space for the reception—and on the customs and wishes of your particular church. You and your florist should always consult the clergyman or someone in the vestry in case there are restrictions.

In your garden or your living room and in most public rooms as well, you generally have to provide some kind of physical focus for the wedding ceremony, an attractive background for the table set up to serve as an altar. Sometimes the garden offers a perfect place—a summerhouse, a pergola, a curving hedge—that may or may not call for additional embellishment. Lacking such space, you can delineate one with tubbed trees or shrubs or create a temporary structure with panels of wooden lattice or metal arches. The latter are widely available—garden-supply catalogues are full of them. They can also be very useful as underpinnings for the decoration of public rooms and tents, and might support vines like ivy or passiflora planted in tubs, or be garlanded with cut vines like smilax or sprengeri and spangled with whatever flowers your fancy chooses. In your living room, the mantelpiece usually offers an easy-to-decorate background for the exchange of vows. But if you don't have one or it is awkwardly placed for that particular purpose, you can call upon that most versatile of furnishings, the folding screen, to create the temporary architecture you need.

The bride married in the Jewish faith has a special space created for her wedding by tradition, whether that wedding takes place in a synagogue, at home, or in a hotel or club. The ceremony is performed under a chuppah, a canopy of cloth or flowers supported on four poles. The chuppah is said to symbolize the new home of the wedded couple. It would be interesting to know if the same meaning was attached to the care cloth, a square of fabric held by four men over the bride and groom at early Anglo-Saxon marriage ceremonies, a custom that lasted well into the sixteenth century in England.

There are endless attractive ways to make chuppahs, or to make a frame for a fabric canopy that is a family heirloom. Sometimes I make a column of twigs around each of the four poles and then tuck into the twigs masses of the tiny white asters called September weed or Montecassino asters in the florist trade.

Other times I swag fabric across the top and then catch it with ribbons in big poufs down the poles. Or I tie up just one pouf with a bow at the top of the pole and then stretch out the fabric in a cone and tack it to the floor. I have also used slender trees as supports and covered their branches with blossoms.

Slender trees can also be used to create a lovely outdoor feeling in a tent even if they are not blossoming trees. Take birches for example. If they don't have to be cut and the root balls can be decoratively wrapped or placed in tubs, you might revive a Tyrolese village custom, whereby each newly married couple plants a tree in the churchyard, or instead plant them in the garden of your new house.

For a Jewish wedding, glossy white bridal satin is swagged over an heirloom chuppah and descends the four posts in conical folds. Caught once in a pouf with satin bow, each tube of satin spreads out at the base as gracefully as the train on the bride's dress. The supporting posts are anchored in cement-filled tubs, and the chuppah is set on a dais at the end of a hotel ballroom. The bride carries a bouquet of white nerines and her veil is caught with a knot of the same blossoms. Photograph by Fred Marcus.

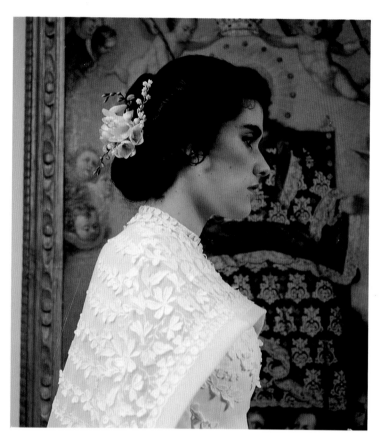 

❧

A Venezuelan bride wears lilies of
the valley and white freesia in her
hair and carries more lilies of the
valley ringed in galax leaves. Her
young attendant's bouquet is a
rosette of galax with a few pink
freesia nestled among the leaves.
All photographs courtesy of
Sagrario Perez-Soto.

☙

Lighting up the wedding reception,
beribboned electric chandeliers
swing from a dead tree "planted"
in the lawn and festooned with
mosses and orchids and *congea
tomentosa*, a mauve and silver vine
from the nearby jungle. It is not a
native, however, but a garden
fugitive from the Orient.

☙

Moss-covered branches sprouting
orchids stand tall on the coffee-
service table and are multiplied to
serve as centerpieces for the
supper tables.

Tables and chairs on the terrace are slipcovered to the floor in white, and pleated white curtains cover the windows at the back for the evening. Moss and orchids drip down from the center of the permanent awning to meet orchids shooting up from the centerpieces, giving the wedding supper a civilized jungle for a background.

The organization and decoration of the wedding reception is really the same as for any large party, and I'll add to my discussion of large parties in the previous chapter only a few points particular to weddings.

Again, please do keep all the professionals helping you informed of everything that is planned. If the bridal cake is going to be brought into the room, around what time is that going to happen? After the luncheon or dinner, after the dance? Will there be toasts? If so at what point, and how long are they expected to last? Who provides the confetti or flower petals to be thrown over the departing couple? We don't use rice any more; birds try to eat what's left on the ground and may die because they can't digest it. Actually, strewing flowers and herbs is nicer and the tradition is just as old. In fact, throwing rice at English and American weddings only began in the 1870s and was probably copied from wedding traditions in India. Throwing grain has always been a symbol of plenty and prosperity, but historically the grain was always the grain grown in the region—wheat, barley, oats—and was often retrieved and sown.

You would not believe how many people bring their wedding presents to the reception, and without putting a card on them! Where do you put them? You should be sure to have one person from the country club or your own household in charge of the presents. And that person should have cards so he or she can write the name of the giver and put it on the present. It is worth hiring someone just to do that if need be. Then afterwards you won't have to suffer the anxiety and embarrassment of not knowing whom to thank for what.

You do want to have a record of your wedding reception. But to have fantastic memories does not mean you have to make it a nightmare for everybody with the kind of overpowering lights used to shoot a commercial movie. They blast out all of the colors, all of the textures, and blind the guests. If you let the photographer become the ringmaster your party will be destroyed: I've seen photographers order or even push people around to get shots. Unless you know a professional photographer who is sensitive and will not destroy the spirit of the occasion, it is really better to have friends or family photograph in a more amateur way.

In some places the bridal table is placed on a dais five or six steps higher than the other tables—rather Renaissancy but not suitable for today. This is often done in Canada, and it puts the guests out of touch with the bride. There is no communication. The whole reception has a more attractive mood if the bride thinks of herself as a hostess, walking among the guests and talking with them and seeing that they are sharing her happiness.

More and more brides today are sharing their happiness by sending the flowers from the church and/or the reception to a hospital or nursing home. Compact center-piece bouquets in mossy or leafy or clear glass containers are very easy to transport. If the bride tells me in advance, and many do, I can often design the room decorations in such a way that they too can be reused. For example, the flowers in a fern garland can be bound together in easily removable sprays or posies. Even very large bouquets can be created in attractive but inexpensive and disposable containers.

Flowery columns and tall candlesticks in alternate pairs flank the red-carpeted aisle for a church wedding in the city. A wooden post covered with water-retaining florist's foam and set in a cement-filled tub for stability constitutes the column's armature. After the gracefully arching ferns and long-stemmed flowers have been placed, moss is attached in strategic spots to disguise the underpinnings. Photographs by Eric Weiss.

Even taller pillars of flowers and ferns frame the altar. For this wedding the flowers include lilies, gerbera, tulips, and orchids in pinks and whites with a few little touches of yellow, but such a decoration can be composed of many different kinds of leaves and flowers, depending on the season and the desired color scheme. At a late autumn ceremony, for example, the columns might be clothed in a combination of bittersweet, autumn leaves, Rothschild lilies, and the smaller sunflowers or gerbera in shades of coral and cream.

Seven different ideas for decorating the center aisle in a church. The two candleholders are freestanding; the rest of the ornaments are built on a commercially available metal or plastic holder for florist's foam that is specifically designed to fit over the edge of the pew. Many churches require the use of such a holder for pew decorations. Photographs by Julio Piedra.

From left to right, a six-foot, three-branch candelabrum is simply garlanded to the floor with beribboned smilax. Next to it and hanging from the pew, fluffy white sweet peas arch over a knot of galax leaves. Suspended from a wide white satin bow, a garland of Queen Anne's lace and smilax is entwined with a streamer of white satin. Roses and ranunculus, lisianthus and lace flowers, sweet peas and hyacinths and freesia surround a 'Stargazer' lily with a burst of glowing color.

A tight nosegay of headily fragrant white lilies, second from left, tops a cascade of smilax and white ribbons. Sprays of white dendrobium orchids curve out from an orchid-starred rosette of galax leaves. Loops of white satin ribbon and a dusting of Queen Anne's lace catch up the smilax hanging from a cluster of white roses at the top of a tall candlestick.

❦

The tent is deliberately almost twice the size needed for 300 guests, which allows for a comfortable generosity of space— and shelter for everyone in case of rain—as well as a passage around the entire perimeter.

❦

The tent on a country house lawn is divided for a wedding reception into a series of open enclosures with arches and railings of birch twigs studded with flowers.

❦

The buffet is at one end of the tent, the dance floor in the center, and surrounding it are bays each holding four tables for eight or ten.

Birch twigs wrapping the center tent poles bush out near the top, almost concealing the electrified candelabra specially designed to fit around the poles.

❧

The posts and rails and gateways
were first constructed in two-by-
twos and then covered in birch
twigs: a week's work for six pairs
of hands. The flowers, in individual water-filled vials camouflaged
with moss, were added at the last
minute.

❧

Alstroemeria, nerines, gerberas,
stock, freesia, brodiaea, and
orchids all contributed blossoms,
but they by no means exhaust the
varieties of flowers that might
have been used to bring accents of
color and fragrance to what is
essentially a black and white decor.

The tables were all skirted to the ground in white cotton moiré.

For the centerpieces, bundles of
twigs tied with raffia at the corners
band square galax-wrapped boxes
filled with water-retaining foam.
"Planted" in the boxes are little
gardens made up of lilies, freesia,
lilies of the valley, brodiaea, and a
single tulip.

CONTAINERS FROM NATURE

Grape hyacinths encircled by asparagus, a design in which container and arrangement are inseparable, takes its inspiration from the formal congruence between flower and vegetable. The asparagus are simply tied on with multicolored cords and can be recycled for the soup kettle after a day or two. Neighbors on the bamboo tabletop are the figure of a Thai holy man, a lacquer frog, a jade tray holding various pieces of gold jewelry, and two chintz-covered votive lights. Photograph by Roger Bester.

When the inspiration for arrangements comes from nature, why not do them in something that nature gives to you? In my flower arrangements I always try to stay with the natural movement of the flowers, the actual structural way that the flowers grow. For example, I try to place flowers in a container so that the stem goes straight down, not at an angle. This sounds as if it would be limiting, even unnecessarily limiting, but it is not. In almost any group of flowers there are some with stems that curve and bend naturally, so you can take advantage of the movement of the flower but still place the stem the way it grows in nature. Even some flowers that appear rather stiff will bend and twist once they have been placed in the container—tulips are a prime example. Or you can achieve movement in your design by controlling the height. Take blossoms with rigid stems like hydrangeas or achilleas, or, for that matter, many hot-house-grown roses. Once in a while you find one with a curved stem, but it doesn't matter if you don't because you can shape your arrangement by adjusting the lengths of the stems. Placing flowers in a container the way they grow in nature is an easy way to avoid the artificiality that puts so many people off the whole idea of flower arranging. And what is more natural to this way of thinking than to base the containers that hold the flowers in nature?

After all, many of the classic shapes of containers come from natural forms. Think of ancient Egyptian pomegranate-inspired bottles, Chinese and Japanese vases shaped like eggplants, mangoes, gourds and double gourds, melons and flower bulbs or sections of bamboo. Fruit and vegetable forms have been repeated by glassblowers, potters, and metalworkers for many centuries in many civilizations. But you can make your own container from the model, the original vegetable. I often hollow out an eggplant or a squash, an artichoke or a gourd just enough to insert a test tube to hold water for a flower or a few. Or if a fruit was the model, the original fruit—smooth watermelons or textured cantaloupes, even pineapples. True, these containers won't last forever, but they will last as long as the flowers in them. And you don't have to find space to store them!

When I use flowers in a crystal vase, I usually separate the vase from the flowers with leaves. They soften the coldness of the crystal, which always seems to me a bit shocking. And from that I've come to think, "Why not surround the vase entirely in natural materials?" From nature I pick my shapes and forms, and from nature I can pick my textures as well. All you need is a simple straight-sided container of the size and shape you want, which you can "slipcover" in the texture of your choice. And the choice is endless. You can pick from vegetables like asparagus, rhubarb, chard, peapods, and beans—green or purple; from grasses and reeds and wheat; from twigs and branches; from bark and lichens; from leaves, fresh or dried. I can't think of a natural material that I wouldn't be able to use in some way.

Flowers and natural elements blend so well. The look of old terra cotta with moss growing on it and flowers coming out of it for me is perfection—it makes everything

After centuries of serving metalworkers, potters, and glassblowers as models, eggplants, squash, and artichokes become containers in their own right. Their stems inserted in glass candleholders and given moss collars with raffia ties, a pair of artichokes raises aloft a pair of pink lilies. An acorn squash in a brass ring holds a nosegay of roses. A large eggplant supports an about-to-bloom amaryllis belladonna, a smaller one is filled with red astrantia, and a third pretends to be a lacquer box. Completing the tablescape, a pair of Chinese jade birds on elaborate stands and a very baroque Brazilian candlestick. In all of these vegetable vases hidden glass tubes or florist's water picks hold the water that the flowers need. Photograph by Guy Lindsay.

❦

Pink hyacinths bedded in sphagnum moss peep out from a moss-and-toadstool grotto built up around the handle of an old willow basket. More toadstools scallop the basket's rim. With all its air of having been scooped up intact from the forest floor this arrangement is actually a careful construction. The toadstools are glued to the basket, the hyacinths are held in position by crushed chickenwire in the liner, and the moss conceals all the mechanics as well as contributing color and texture to the design. Photograph by Peter Margonelli.

look so fresh, so natural. But, much as I love it, I have not yet succeeded in making moss grow on a terra-cotta container inside the house the way it does outside or in the greenhouse. I often do cover metal or plastic containers with moss; it's also a look I'm very fond of, but it's not the same.

Baskets are classic containers from nature. The first thing you do when you cut flowers usually is put them in a basket. And I suspect that baskets were one of the earliest containers used for flowers: baskets of blossoms carried to a temple, garlands of flowers heaped in baskets. We can see baskets of fruit and lotus blossoms in Egyptian tomb paintings and baskets of flowers in Roman mosaics. So many wonderful flower paintings show baskets used as containers, over and over in every century and all around the world.

The big problem today is finding proper liners for baskets. It has become terribly expensive to have metal liners made, if indeed you can find anyone to make them. But you can almost always find among the various sizes and shapes in housewares departments plastic containers that will fit. Just be sure that the container is made of a kind of plastic that you can really keep clean, that is, wash in very, very hot water. Also, disposable paint buckets are cheap and available in many sizes. If the color isn't quite right you can always spray on a coat of paint or tuck leaves between container and basket—a trick often shown in eighteenth-century French flower paintings.

We often think of baskets for country or rustic arrangements, but baskets go very well on a formal table, especially for period arrangements. Unless you have the proper cachepot or porcelain bowl for an eighteenth-century bouquet, it is better to use a basket. Appropriate shapes for the period are very easy to find. You can mix a basket with silver, you can mix a basket with gold. And the shapes are wonderful.

A ruffly red mound of cockscomb
celosia fringed with galax leaves
fills a birchbark canister. Dried,
the celosia will not be as brilliant,
but its softer tones will be equally
appealing. Table companions are a
dancing blanc-de-chine boatman
and an even whiter Chinese
porcelain bowl. Photograph by
Guy Lindsay.

Grapevines loosely woven into a large rustic basket embrace a fresh composition in greens and whites. Pale green grapes, soft green moss, and shiny dark green galax leaves set off individual buds and blossoms of the Christmas rose, *Helleborus niger*, and ranunculus; sprays of lily of the valley and freesia; delicate umbels of Queen Anne's lace; dense hyacinth spikes; and one splendid 'Casa Blanca' lily. Each blossom in this arrangement is treated as an individual and its special qualities emphasized by the framing galax leaves, an approach that works best when the flowers are all of a color. Pink or yellow versions could still contain lilies, ranunculus, freesia, and hyacinths—although yellow hyacinths are not common—but substitutes would be needed for the Christmas roses, the Queen Anne's lace, and the lily of the valley. As long as the choice of flowers offers a variety of textures and forms it need not duplicate those in this arrangement. The foundation is simply crushed chickenwire in the basket's liner. Photograph by Peter Margonelli.

🖤

Light-hearted flowers, serious decoration. A sheaf of cornflowers in a glass cylinder wrapped in a sheaf of wheat cinched with a fat raffia knot shares an eighteenth-century Chinese lacquer table with a carved carnelian persimmon, an eighteenth-century French sewing kit or necessaire, and one of a pair of Meissen pug dogs. Next to the table a seventeenth-century Flemish historical tapestry, and above it an eighteenth-century Dutch marine scene. The living-room was designed by Lourdes Catão. Photograph by Guy Lindsay.

Baskets do just what we are talking about when we speak of containers from nature, they bring a natural element to the arrangement. Somehow, even when they display an enormous amount of skill and creativity as some intricate Japanese baskets do, the material seems to keep its essential character. It is still bamboo, or willow, or grapevine. There's just a little more handwork involved. This is a fine line, I admit. You could say that all containers come from nature. The clay, the sand and silica, the metallic ores are all materials from nature. The difference is the amount of human intervention needed.

The nice thing when you use natural elements is to let them be natural—don't treat them too much, don't work on them too much, use them for the beauty that they have. If you work them, polish them too much, they become something else. Then you're not dealing with nature, you're dealing with craft. There's a difference between craft-made pieces and things made by nature. The one is a permanent entity with its own character which preceded and will outlive the arrangement; the other is an integral part of the design and will last only as long as the design does. It is not a question of better or worse, but there is a nice feeling in doing something for an occasion or a guest that's so special it won't survive.

Selma Zebrina beans strung on wires sash a container lapped with galax leaves. The very mixed bouquet includes white hydrangeas, amaryllis belladonna, lily buds, scabiosa, and roses of cream, apricot, orange, and bright red. The frog harnessed to a shell is an *objet de virtu* by Marguerite Stix; the silver porringer is seventeenth-century Dutch. Photograph by Guy Lindsay.

Red and greenish-white mottled Selma Zebrina beans, topped and tailed and tied with red silk cord, turn a simple plastic cylinder into a very decorative holder for a galax-frilled nosegay of creamy pink roses and pale lavender sweet peas. The silver saucer is seventeenth-century Dutch, the frog Chinese. Photograph by Guy Lindsay.

A study in color and texture for a day's pleasure. Perfectly matched scallions encircle massed half-open flower clusters of Autumn Joy sedum. A Chinese celadon charger and two lacquered wood canisters from India complete the still-life. Very fresh scallions will last a day without giving off an obtrusive odor, and they need not go to waste once they've served their decorative duty, since they are simply tied around a plastic cylinder that has been wrapped in a thin sheet of foam. Photograph by Guy Lindsay.

153

A few cultivated double rudbeckias invade an informal gathering of meadow flowers composed of their wild cousins, the black-eyed Susans, and dainty white erigeron, also known as fleabane. A layer of soft green moss camouflages the container inside the bamboo basket. Sheathing the liner of an openwork basket with moss or leaves is a traditional way to bring basket and flowers into natural harmony—some eighteenth-century engravings even show blossoms tucked among the leaves. Photograph by Marisa Alvarez Lima.

Clusters of eucalyptus buds and paperwhite narcissus blossoms spill over a circular hedge of dried lavender belted with green grosgrain. A lavender-covered container like this might have started out fresh and blue and green, to hold garden pinks and forget-me-nots. Then, as the lavender dried and its colors paled, it might have been host to pink, white, and green nicotiana, and finally ended the year with the winter arrangement illustrated. Photograph by Peter Margonelli.

❧

Adjusting container to background, pencil-thin bamboo canes cinched with raffia encircle a plastic container. More reeds cut and tied with raffia simulate a handle, creating a Japonesque basket for a nosegay of roses, lilies, and deep purple lisianthus. The handle is purely decorative, inserted in the foam that fills the container just as the flower stems are, but the arrangement is nevertheless a highly portable one. Photograph by Marisa Alvarez Lima.

❧

A basket constructed from slices of bamboo laced together with caning strips—sides, bottom, and handles alike—holds a bud vase bouquet of astroemeria, grape hyacinths, freesia, and miniature lilies plus a scented candle in a soapstone caddy tied with raffia. Ready to travel and a perfect hostess present, but temptingly easy to find a place for in your own house. Photograph by Marisa Alvarez Lima.

❧

The reed-like stems of horsetail, equisetum, turn a plastic container into a finely fluted column for the jaunty pink and white plumes of a member of the amaranth family called by florists wheat celosia. This arrangement could have a good long life, since both horsetail and celosia dry very well. Another easy-to-dry flower that would find such a container becoming is globe amaranth or gomphrena. Photograph by Guy Lindsay.

DESIGNS FOR THE HOLIDAY SEASON

❦

Three sober little wood-colored angels trailing clouds of glorious silver and gold lamé provide a triumphantly festive frame for an equally festive dining table. Lamé bows at the four corners tie a square blue moiré cloth into swags over a round table for two skirted to the floor in orange moiré. More lamé bows diffuse the light from the center lantern and the whole table service sparkles with gold. Party dress for the boxwood topiary centerpiece: garlands and plumes of white dendrobium orchids. Photograph by Peter Margonelli.

 *A*lmost every month in the year has at least one holiday, one person or one event to commemorate, and some months have several. But when anyone says holiday, what comes to my mind is the period that begins in November with Thanksgiving and only comes to a close with the New Year. I suspect that most people feel the same, whether the high point of their holiday season is Christmas or Hanukkah. In this country we don't extend our celebrations until Twelfth Night, January 6, as is the custom in many European countries, but then Europeans don't start as early as we do: Thanksgiving is strictly North American as an official holiday, even if it does follow in the age-old tradition of harvest festivals.

The season's sense of sharing, of giving and receiving, puts everyone in a hospitable mood, eager to entertain friends and family. We really decorate our houses for these holidays. It's wonderful because there are so many places that you can decorate, and you have so much freedom to express yourself in the holiday dress that you give your house. You can be childlike, you can be serious; you can be stylized or nostalgic; and you can choose to interpret any traditions that appeal to you.

A celebration to give thanks for a bountiful harvest suggests first of all ideas for decorating the table, and it is generally a centerpiece for a festive meal that we want to create for

A sweet-faced papier-mâché cherub colored to look like carved wood wears a chaplet of moss and dried roses on his head. His matching offering of moss and roses is built on a chicken-wire frame. Although the roses that are dried to retain their color often come with stems intact, the stems are too stiff to bend into graceful curves. Here, as happens more often than not, the blossoms have been removed to be glued or wired in a pleasing design to an appropriate foundation. Photograph by Peter Margonelli.

Thanksgiving. Sheaves of wheat are a classic: standing tall and simply tied with ribbon, or wreathed with bittersweet, or centering a pile of colorful fruits and vegetables. Fruits—apples, winter pears, persimmons—stacked in pyramids need only bits of moss or a soft dried flower like statice tucked in between to help them keep their balance. If the form really appeals to you, it is worth looking in shops or catalogues or flea markets for the pyramidal wire forms made specifically to hold fruit. They can be filled with peaches in summer, pomegranates at Christmas, and oranges or lemons any time of year. I also like to have bowls of fruit and nuts and candies all over the house throughout the holiday season. A big silver bowl heaped with pomegranates or shiny red apples or my favorite, pomanders—oranges or lemons or even apples studded with cloves and sprinkled with spices. The mingling of fruit with cloves and cinnamon gives a wonderfully warm and welcoming scent to a room.

From long before the beginning of history, midwinter in the northern hemisphere has been a season of festivals and holidays. It may also have been for the inhabitants of the lands below the tropic of Capricorn as well. After all, in an agricultural society it is a time of year with time for celebrating. Whatever the difference in place, epoch, or religious belief, all winter solstice celebrations have included sun worship and revels, lights and plants, and, at least since we have records, all have been remarkably hospitable to ideas and images from other cultures. According to the Venerable Bede, writing at the end of the seventh century A.D., December 25 was a feast day in ancient Britain long before it was officially designated, in the late fourth century, as the birthday of the Christ Child. Another ancestor of our holiday season, the successive Roman festivals called *Saturnalia, Dies Natalis Solis Invicti, Calendae Ianuari,* began on December 17

🐦

A buffet-sized tabletop tree in soft
greens and pinks is constructed of
box branches and PeeGee
hydrangea panicles with their
stems inserted in a rigid foam
cone. What look like shiny pink
leaves are the calyxes of the
familiar red Chinese lanterns,
Physalis franchetii, cut in half and
dried. Dried red rosebuds and
gold lamé ribbon bows dangling
small silver pendants give accents
of color and glitter. Originally
created for Mme Moreira Salles,
it now shares the sideboard in this
fabric-tented dining room with a
pair of seventeenth-century
Brazilian candlesticks and a huge
hand of bananas to balance the
bowl of Thai carved wood bananas
and tropical fruits on top of the
marbleized column. For fragrance,
flats of paperwhite narcissus
guarded by a Brazilian folk-art
lion fill the door to the
conservatory. The painting is by
Roberto Burle Marx and the room
was decorated by James O'Brien.
Photograph by Guy Lindsay.

and lasted through the first week of January. Saturnalia, originally a feast marking the
end of the autumn sowing, became a seven-day spree of garlanding and festooning,
caroling and masquerading, present-giving and feasting, and free speech for slaves.
Over time it acquired a reputation for licentious excess; but the December 25 religious celebration, borrowed from Persia, of the Birth of the Unconquered Sun gave
the Christian church a perfect pretext—had not the Evangelists called Jesus "the
light of the world"?—for redirecting the whole joyous interval and many of its customs to commemorate a sacred event.

We always seem to think of Christmas as being red and white or red and green,
which I suppose is natural in those parts of the world where the land is covered with
snow and the most common colors nature provides are evergreen greens and berry
reds: rose hips, holly berries, barberries, winterberries. But we shouldn't feel limited
to these colors; other combinations may be more attractive in your house or simply
seem more festive to you. And you can experiment with different shades and tones of
these traditional colors. Deeper reds like bordeaux or brick, or rosy shades don't grab
your eyes like the traditional Christmas red but they blend better into most rooms.
And rich dark colors need not seem somber: all they need is a touch of gold or silver to
pep them up.

Spring colors, too, are wonderful for the holidays. They're not seasonal, I know,
and although I generally prefer to stay with the colors and flowers of the season, there
is something irresistible about the tints and scents of spring in the darkest days of the
year. Paperwhite narcissus and amaryllis are becoming as associated with the holidays
as the more difficult-to-use poinsettias, which to my mind always look better in really

❦

Another and differently shaped hydrangea and boxwood tree is set in a simple basket. To achieve this particular form it is built up on a chickenwire armature. None of the ingredients need water—the roses have been dried by a method that keeps their colors brilliant, and the box and the hydrangeas will dry naturally. Photographs by Guy Lindsay.

❦

Close up you can really appreciate the subtle colors of the drying hydrangeas, ranging from violet through pink and pale green to soft beige in the thoroughly dry ones, and enjoy the intricate workmanship in the silver and gold-washed Indian ornaments that hang from gold lamé ribbon bows all over the tree.

A versatile holiday table ornament, this boxwood ball elevated on a bundle of branches above a boxwood hemisphere in a terra-cotta cube is studded with tiny, shiny tree ornaments, its Christmas guise. For Thanksgiving it might sport the smallest of pumpkins or lady apples or nuts, natural or gilded, or a constellation of daisies. Photograph by Peter Margonelli.

It's not a Christmas tree, but the similarity of form and the incrustation of moss and dried red roses make this marbleized wood obelisk on a white-washed miniature terra-cotta Versailles box seem like a holiday ornament. It might center a table for two or four, or with a twin, garnish a mantelpiece. Moss and roses can be cemented to the wood with epoxy if you want them permanent, casein glue if you want them removable. Photograph by Peter Margonelli.

large spaces like lobbies and ballrooms. Narcissus and amaryllis are almost foolproof and you can force the bulbs yourself even in apartments with far from ideal conditions. Not much more demanding are the specially prepared lily-of-the-valley pips; but hyacinths, tulips, iris, and lilies are better bought in bloom unless you have an evenly cool dark room and then a sunny window in which to coax them into flower.

The range of spring flowers we have to choose from has been enormously increased in the last few years, but the idea of forcing spring blossoms for Christmas is not a new one. It was common in nineteenth-century households that had greenhouses and gardeners; and historians tell us that at least as far back as the sixteenth century, German families were forcing fruit tree boughs for holiday decoration. Christmas carols and Christmas lore are full of trees that mysteriously burst into bloom at Christmastime. The English legend of the Glastonbury thorn, the hawthorn staff carried by Joseph of Arimathea that bloomed overnight and still blooms every year at Christmas, is just one of them.

Christmas trees filled with flowers are one of my favorite fantasies, and I was delighted to learn from Phillip V. Snyder's *The Christmas Tree Book* (New York, 1976) that roses were the first Christmas tree ornaments. The earliest Christmas trees of which we have written accounts were recorded in the Baltic cities of Riga and Reval in the early 1500s, and in Strasbourg less than a century later, and all were decorated with roses made of paper. We don't have to use artificial ones anymore: water-picks will keep fresh ones fresh and new techniques have made it possible to dry roses so that they keep most of their color.

You don't have to search for a precedent in history to justify out-of-the-ordinary

A pair of truly fastigiate common junipers borne on the backs of Thai temple boys in lacquered wood frame a living room window. These living Christmas trees are planted in terra-cotta pots which have been padded, wrapped in striped lamé, and belted with red silk cord to resemble oriental cushions. Bows and streamers of the same lamé, fragrant rosebud-studded foam balls suspended from gold cords, and contemporary Neapolitan crèche angels provide the decoration. Two flats of paperwhite narcissus add still more perfume. A collection of antique Persian pottery and a pair of Chinese jade birds fill the side table in this living room decorated by James O'Brien. The gilt-wood mirrors are Venetian, the celadon charger and figurines, Chinese. Photograph by Guy Lindsay.

In another incarnation of the same living room, one of the Venetian mirrors hangs over the fireplace. Glass bud vases holding single tulips and umbels of Queen Anne's lace line up on top of the mantle along with rose-swagged moss topiaries in terra-cotta pots and votive candles on brass candlesticks. Around them and down the sides of the mantle sweep bows and streamers of gold lamé scarfing a moss teddy bear and garlanding a bundle of kindling. Photograph by Peter Margonelli.

tree ornaments, but you could probably find one for almost anything, since tree-worship is so ancient and decorated trees so much a part of winter solstice celebrations in all cultures. A "great tree decorated with jewels" was one of the lures offered by the other gods to entice the Sun Goddess from the cave in which she had taken refuge in a charming ancient Japanese myth related by Joseph Campbell. And the Persian king Cyrus is said to have garlanded his favorite tree with golden chains.

Our eyes seem to long for green in winter. You want to see green inside the house because you can't see it outside the house. Whether we look out on snow and ice or mud and bare branches or sunburnt Mediterranean hillsides, the presence of green seems a magical refreshment, and many plants and trees that stay green all winter have lovely scents. Sometimes I think that all I need to decorate for the holidays are greens—just one kind or a blend of many shades and textures. You can even find greens that will look attractive in a dark green room. That is tricky, because dye or paint colors tend to fight with natural colors, but there is sure to be one that will work at either the yellowish or the bluish end of the green spectrum. You can make wonderful garlands of mixed greens—snippets of familiar Christmas evergreens like pine, fir, spruce, juniper, box, and yew; of sturdy herbs like thyme and rosemary and bay; and of garden evergreens that rarely appear on the florists' market like camellia, cotoneaster, euonymus, kalmia, pieris, pittosporum, rhododendron. As you wire them around lengths of sturdy twine you may tuck in some sprays of heather or perhaps even a few holly twigs, although they are a bit too spiky to use in quantity. This only begins to suggest the materials you can use to compose garlands and wreaths, which are made much the same way but built on a rigid rather than a flexible framework.

Flanked by crystal candlesticks and an arrangement of Chinese glazed pottery fruit that includes an exotic Buddha's hand, a Christmas wreath designed to enchant the nose as well as the eye. Fresh pink roses and dried pink rosebuds, clusters of eucalyptus buds, bundles of cinnamon sticks, and a tangle of aromatic vetiver roots all wrapped up and tied with gauzy gold ribbon compose an unexpected potpourri that needs only a good spritz of water to send its spicy scent around the room. Waterpicks inserted in the moss-covered chicken-wire foundation keep the roses supplied with water; the rose leaves don't need it, they are artificial. Photograph by Guy Lindsay.

A wreath of feathery incense cedar hangs like a trophy from a many-streamered bowknot of gold lamé ribbon. Another bow and more ribbons thread through the aromatic branches. The cedar has a fringe of darker green yew, and both evergreens are wired to a wire wreath form. On the mantleshelf a Chinese parrot on one side is balanced by a pair of antique brass candlesticks with a Chinese porcelain bowl between them. Photograph by Guy Lindsay.

White heather tied with a silver lamé bow to make a giant version of the wreath worn by emperors and athletic champions in classical antiquity. The foundation is a plump ring of yew clippings wired around a metal ring into which the heather stems are inserted in overlapping layers. In the holiday season it is quite often possible to buy simple evergreen wreaths from Christmas-tree vendors, and these could be elaborated in the same way. The mantel decoration is completed by a pair of antique English wood and pewter candlesticks and a quill basket holding Indian ornamental balls carved from horn. Photograph by Guy Lindsay.

Every climate, every part of the world has beautiful local materials. Throwing imitation snow over artificial spruce trees in the tropics is ridiculous. If you are in the tropics, create a tropical Christmas. You can still decorate trees, indigenous trees, and you can still make wreaths and garlands. You don't have to have pine, you can use native vines or straw or wheat or beautiful grasses. You can have the same kind of color and movement, but with materials appropriate to the place. Once I did a wedding anniversary party in Caracas three or four weeks before Christmas, and all the decorations I did were left in place for Christmas: garlands of rosemary, garlands of sweet grass with dried flowers and ribbons in very bright colors threaded through them.

According to historians, celebrants in the ancient Jewish winter festival that was the ancestor of Hanukkah wore wreaths of ivy and carried boughs and palm branches. Today we tend to think of Hanukkah as a festival of lights and for very good reason. With the transformation of the ancient celebration into a commemoration of the retaking of the Temple in Jerusalem by the Maccabees in the second century before Christ came a tradition that I find one of the loveliest of the holiday season: the lighting of the candles, a ceremony that honors the single miraculous vial of sanctified oil that burned for the eight days of the reconsecration of the temple. On each of the eight nights of Hanukkah an additional candle on the nine-branch candelabrum called a menorah is lighted from the central candle as prayers are said. Traditional songs are sung, traditional foods served. For the children in the family there are traditional games to play and on each of the nights each of them is given a small present. Traditional colors are blue and silver, but you can use most of the same materials for

In a ceremony at the core of Hanukkah, the Jewish Festival of Lights, one candle is lighted each day from the central one on the nine-branch candelabrum called a menorah until all are burning, as they are on this leafy menorah. The metal candelabrum was specially designed to hold votive lights and to be covered in flowers or foliage. Here it is clothed in boxwood with sprays of heather radiating from a silver lamé bow—blue and silver are the traditional Hanukkah colors. Sprigs of juniper would be another attractive choice, especially if they were heavily laden with blue berries, or, indeed, so would any of the evergreens with glaucous needles. In the southern states, such a menorah might be covered with one of the silvery foliages like artemisia, dusty miller, santolina, or even olive branchlets. Photograph by Guy Lindsay.

❦

A rose-covered haystack for a Christmas tree? But there was hay in the manger and Renaissance Christmas trees were decorated with roses, albeit of paper. Here, the roses are real but dried; the hay is what is called salt or marsh hay, which is sold to cover plants in winter; and the tree is built on a moss-covered chicken-wire armature. Gold ribbon bows dangling tiny silver whirligigs catch up the swirling hay in random tufts.

❦

Same ingredients, a very different result: a moss and hay pagoda encrusted with rosebuds. True, it is raffia, not ribbon, that ties the graduated rings of hay into upcurving bundles. Both of these hay trees demand considerable skill—hay is not easy to handle, although it is somewhat less brittle when dampened—but their attractiveness emphasizes the importance of being open to the unexpected potential of the materials around us. Photographs by Peter Margonelli.

decorations as you do for Christmas, because most of them have more to do with winter than with religion.

What's important is to keep the childlike quality in holiday celebrations. It's a time for burning logs and lights and candles and reflections. All kinds of shiny sparkly things, sequins and tinsel and glittering ornaments, things that at any other time would be a bit gaudy go with the joy of the season. At Christmas I love the sheen of gold and silver in fabrics and ribbons and ornaments, and in silver bowls of gold and silver Jordan almonds scattered around the house. Spontaneity, generosity, renewal, happiness—these are the great traditions of the season.

Apples, pears, bananas, and grapes heaped up in a two-foot pyramid and surmounted by that classic symbol of hospitality, the pineapple, invite guests to the Thanksgiving table. Standing in for stiffer wheat as a harvest representative, tufts of dried maiden grass, *Miscanthus sinensis* 'Gracillimus', spurt up in graceful arcs between the fruits; galax leaves and ivy sprigs add a dash of green; and tendrils of Spanish moss ensure that the rigid foam cone supporting this bounty remains unseen. Equally invisible: the wooden picks that attach fruit and foliage to the foam. Miniaturizing such an arrangement for a smaller table is easy now that tiny pineapples, no more than four inches top to stem tip, are readily available in autumn and winter. Other lilliputian elements might include lady apples, limes and kumquats or clementines, pearl-sized champagne grapes, finger bananas, small-leafed ivies like 'Digitata' or 'Minima', and any number of fine dried grasses. Photograph by Roger Bester.

An apple-bearing boxwood bush, criss-crossed with gold ribbon and the golf-ball-like blossoms of silver brunia and tightly girdled with cinnamon sticks, makes a highly aromatic holiday table decoration, and one that could move back and forth with ease between dining and coffee tables. The cinnamon sticks are first glued to a plastic box, then tied with ribbon. The bush is built from box clippings set in water-retaining foam. Photographs by Peter Margonelli.

In a variation on the cinnamon-bound boxwood theme, the container is round instead of square; the boxwood has a border of gold and silver ribbons twisted together; and more ribbons wreathe the center apple and wind through a circle of silver brunia blossoms. The apples need not be attached, so there's no need to say "Don't eat the centerpiece."

To create all-out glamour for a gala dinner in a New York apartment, tables are sheathed in cloth-of-gold and the chimney breast wreathed in Rococo festoons of golden gauze swagged and draped from a curtain rod above the mirror. Over them, narrow gold and mauve and pink ribbons swing from a center panache of gold and silver paper fans. Photographs by Edgar De Evia, courtesy of *House & Garden*.

On the tables, dancing circles of delicate white lace flowers spring from moss-bound test tubes partially implanted in artichokes and apples. More apples, lady apples flourishing place card arrows, and votive candles in clear faceted glasses complete the table decoration.

❦

Held firmly in a two-dimensional
fan, sixteen stems of *Brodiaea laxa*,
a summer-blooming California
native, look for all the world like
something from an Egyptian wall
painting. Two thin slices of green
bamboo tied together clasp the
flower umbels, two slightly shorter
ones wound with raffia separate
the stems in the center, and a
third, still shorter, adds visual
balance at the mouth of the
Japanese bronze vase. Photograph
courtesy of Gumps.

*C*an you imagine anyone who wouldn't be thrilled to hear people say "What a wonderful arrangement! So original! I've never seen anything like it before!" But you or I, he or she, ought to be concerned rather than complimented if those exclamations don't include a "How attractive! How lovely! How beautiful!"

Astonishment, surprise, individuality certainly have an appeal. But simply trying to be original may produce something never seen before, which might well be something neither you nor anyone else ever wants to see again.

In any case, originality doesn't seem to me a very important goal when you are working with flowers: what you are trying to do is bring nature into the house in the most appealing possible way, whether you are doing it for your own pleasure, or, as a professional, for the pleasure of others. You don't set out to create a style, but as you become better and better at giving form to those feelings your arrangements tend to take on an individual personality. You find certain rhythms and proportions more satisfying than others. Some color combinations please you, others don't. Certain shapes, certain kinds of construction turn out to be particularly sympathetic. I am especially fond of good old traditions like topiary work that can be applied to the modern age. And we all have our favorite flowers.

❦

Moss gives topiary shapes a lovely velvety green coat, but for a true moss-lover that is only the beginning. A mossy globe garlanded with dried rosebuds "grows" up from a moss bed in a moss-covered terra-cotta pot. Even its birch-branch stem sports a collar of moss tied on with a raffia bow. Color-matched but not moss-backed, a rose-bearing frog completes the composition. It usually takes both glue and a reinforcing wrap of fine green wire to attach moss to a terra-cotta pot or a hard plastic foam sphere. Photograph by Peter Margonelli.

As I organized the pictures for this book I realized that there are certain shapes or ideas that I keep coming back to—baskets with handles, topiary balls, moss-covered forms, and single flowers—and I have gathered several examples of each for this chapter to illustrate my feelings about the evolution of personal style. Also, much as I love and love to make informal garden bouquets which, if you let the flowers take their natural bent, are never twice the same, I have never ceased to be fascinated by the kind of controlled arrangement that expresses a flower's rhythm in a very stylized way. These are represented here as well. From time to time, one or another of these favorites falls out of favor for a while. Then I see a new-to-me leaf or flower that I'd like to try in topiary form or I decide to cover hearts instead of bears with moss or I think of a better way to make a basket. If you are always open to anything that might be offered as material to work with, you will always find fresh challenges and fresh ways to perfect your visual ideas. Style, originality, and the surprise they produce are simply a by-product of trying to do your best.

But you do have to begin somewhere. When I first started giving flower-arranging demonstrations, I was trying to tell people what you can do with flowers. Usually, most of the time was devoted to taking apart arrangements I had brought to show how they were constructed; showing what a flower arrangement is rather than how to make a flower arrangement. Then I realized that that was not quite fair. I was not really giving my audiences the guidance they wanted. In a way, when I talk about what other people can do, it's a kind of shorthand and I'm assuming that they have the same kind of vision I have. It's not correct for me to assume that everybody sees the way that I see. Now I start right out, "This is what I do. This is where I begin."

Topiary work, the clipping and training of shrubs or trees into geometric forms or green animals, is at least as old as the Roman Empire. It's a tradition that has never totally disappeared from the garden world, even though condemned from time to time as unnatural by changing fashion. Today we seem to find arrangements of leaves or flowers in topiary form equally at home in traditional and modern rooms.

❧

Table decorations lifted, and miniaturized, from topiary-filled seventeenth- and eighteenth-century formal gardens have been popular off and on since those centuries, when they were even copied in gold and silver. Here, an unclipped ball-on-stem boxwood topiary ringed by a circular hedge of clipped boxwood centers a round table set for four in a dining room decorated by James O'Brien and with murals by Michael Klaric. If regularly spritzed, these components made of florist's-foam-fixed boxwood clippings compose long-lasting and adaptable centerpieces. All in green, they calmly complement any color scheme; with a scattering of tucked-in blossoms—it doesn't take very many—they play a more dynamic color role. Photograph by Guy Lindsay.

To create a full-fledged parterre
in the center of an oval table, the
two halves of the circular hedge
are separated and a pair of clipped
ball-on-stem topiaries in tiny
Versailles boxes are joined by four
rectangular hedges. Elements of
this kind can be arranged in any
number of patterns to suit
different sizes and shapes of table.
The foundations for these hedge
pieces are florist's foam covered
with artificial galax leaves, but sets
of containers to serve the same
purpose do appear on the market
from time to time, usually made of
china or glass. Artificial galax
leaves also sheathe the votive
candles that light the dinner table
set with Tobacco Leaf china,
English silver flatware and
Baccarat crystal. The dining room,
papered with Zuber murals of
Brazilian scenes by Rugendas, was
designed by Lourdes Catão.
Photograph by Guy Lindsay.

We are always looking for inspiration, all of us. In talking about flower arranging as an art form I have suggested several sources, foremost among them Nature, at once the most profound and most accessible inspiration source we have. Her shapes and colors, her unpredictable combinations are a never-ending surprise. But there are technical considerations to be mastered in translating an idea from the natural world into a workable flower arrangement. Those of us who write books and give lectures can help, and not just with practical tips. Seeing how someone else has given concrete form to his vision can be enormously helpful in clarifying yours and finding the form for it or in breaking out of a certain approach that no longer seems satisfying. That master stylist, Marcel Proust, once suggested in an essay that deliberately writing a short piece in the manner of a writer you admired was the most effective way to learn from another writer. Copying an arrangement that you admire is one way and a good one to learn the craft.

There is very, very little, if indeed there is anything, that is truly new. Occasionally I've felt that I had come up with a new idea for constructing an arrangement, only to notice months later something almost identical in a Renaissance painting. It seems we all tend to solve certain kinds of problems the same way. It really doesn't matter where an idea comes from as long as it is a good idea. The key that turns inspiration into creation is to do better something that was done before, whether you did it before or someone else did. But to respond creatively in whatever medium you choose, you have to understand your medium's qualities and respect its possibilities and limitations.

As you arrange the same kinds of flowers over and over again you keep gaining confidence. It seems almost as if nature makes them grow in your hands. The more you use any material, the more you will learn about the kind of treatment it demands,

Almost more trellis than handle, bamboo stakes lashed together with raffia splay out from the interior of a wooden box. The composition combines primrose plants, paperwhite narcissus bulbs, and cut stems of lavender freesia, white ranunculus, and paperwhite narcissus. Photograph by Marisa Alvarez Lima.

*E*xtreme abstractions of the natural rhythms to be found in plants and flowers can make amusing, even witty arrangements. The danger to be avoided is a sense of strain, of forcing the stems or blossoms into an unnatural pattern.

❧

An elaborate arrangement of containers lined up on a Japanese black lacquer footed tray is composed of three double gourd crystal vases yoked by long glass rods tied with narrow gold ribbon bows. A short-stemmed white rose standing straight in each vase acts as counterpoint to the diagonal rhythm of freesia stems, tied where they cross with Spanish moss-buffered raffia bows. Photograph by Roger Bester.

A trio of opaline glass bud vases on an ebony platform holds six stems of star-of-Bethlehem tied into a diagonal design with raffia bows. The result is very reminiscent of what is called a Belgian fence espalier, a method of pruning fruit trees both for decorative effect and to increase fruit production when space is limited. Photograph courtesy of Gumps.

❦

A simple glass globe slip-covered in cream-colored faille to blend with a Brazilian artisan's bamboo and papier-maché candleholder and mirror stand holds a mixed bouquet of roses, lilies, grape hyacinths, snowball viburnum, an African daisy, and a calendula. With a supply of fabric squares in different colors—seventeen-inch napkins are perfect for the six-inch size—you can ring endless changes on a few glass spheres, and adjust container to flowers and setting rather than the reverse. Nor do you have to stick to spherical containers. A square of fabric will also cover a cylindrical container, in which case you can use a rubber band to hold the fabric up while you arrange the folds and then conceal it with ribbon or raffia tied in a bow. Photograph by Roger Bester.

the kinds of forms and shapes that are natural to it. When I started making containers wrapped in fabric my designs were very slim, very controlled. Then as I became more accustomed to the body and movement of the fabric they became more lush, more full in volume, softer in shape.

When you know you can do something well, then you can be bolder: push it over, use unexpected elements in unexpected places. Whether or not a daring idea works depends to a very large extent on the quality of its execution.

Changes in decorative fashion over the last twenty years, I do have to say, also helped direct the evolution of my own way of doing things. Would I have considered using multicolored, striped, or patterned fabrics to cover flower containers at the beginning? I very much doubt it. But it now seems perfectly natural to do so because we have become so accustomed to seeing complex mixtures of patterns and colors in rooms. I don't think anyone's way of seeing can resist being influenced to some degree by the spirit of the times. And that's not a bad thing: it pushes you to experiment. You may surprise yourself as well as others with the results you come to by experimenting.

Unceasing experimentation is crucial for those of us for whom arranging and decorating with flowers is a profession. Clients rarely want their party to look like someone else's party. And you are always striving to achieve the right balance between the arrangement you feel works best for the kind of flowers available at a given moment and the kind of arrangement that will look best in a client's room. When you fix flowers for your own pleasure in your own house the pressure is off. The continual practice that is the secret of perfecting your flower arranging skills is the most enjoyable way to spend time I can think of, and I feel that I am very lucky to be able to earn my living by living with flowers.

A bevy of lady's slippers shares a plastic flowerpot that has been transformed into something out of a Turkish harem with foam padding and striped chintz carefully gathered and glued to the rim. The blossoms of the three different orchid varieties are gently tethered to bamboo canes by raffia bows padded with tufts of moss to stabilize the design.

Fabric as a medium for turning very simple and inexpensive globes and cylinders into containers with personality and impact has many possibilities. As these examples show, varying degrees of permanence can be achieved, but none of these containers is likely to survive to heirloom status—nor should it. The point is change. Photographs by Marisa Alvarez Lima.

Arranged in even more pillowy folds, the same many-colored striped chintz cushions a bouquet of godetia, freesia, brodiaea, and sweet peas in shades from deepest plum to palest pink. Inside the wrappings of foam and fabric is a plastic cylinder which holds the water for a dense assemblage of blossoms or water-retaining foam to support a more open design.

A soft container of another stripe holds a shaggy patchwork of pink and red roses and peonies splashed with white freesia and lilies, the last-named barely visible in the photograph. Padded, puffy fabric covers of this kind are made of circles cut to measure and permanently glued to their underlying containers, the raw edge concealed by a glued-on ribbon or bias band of the same fabric. It is not a form of construction that lends itself to last-minute improvisation; it takes some study and practice to execute well.

One of the delights that flows from a mastery of one's materials is the ability to respond with a fresh and unexpected idea to an inspiration suggested by new surroundings or by some aspect of a familiar environment that one had not focused on before.

❦

With some contrivance, the palm trees from the Zuber wallpaper murals of Brazilian scenes come to life in the center of the dining-room table. Palmetto leaves in the market do not have long enough stems to create a proper overarching umbrella, so they are neatly tied with raffia to flexible bamboo canes, along with sprays of white dendrobium orchids. This fantasy interpretation is firmly anchored in a container stuffed with chicken wire under a moss cover and clothed in galax leaves. On the table, set for champagne and about-to-arrive caviar, an array of George III silver and a Bulgari minaudiere reflect and re-reflect the candle flames. The gilded and ebonized inlaid table is English Regency, as are the chairs in this dining room decorated by Lourdes Catão. Photograph by Guy Lindsay.

❦

A spur of the moment site-specific arrangement transforms a graceful bronze maiden into a wood nymph from the grove beyond the window. Garlands of sprengeri stream from her upraised right arm and more sprengeri back the cascade of peach-colored floribunda roses clasped in her left arm. Her usual pedestal replaced by a mossy birch stump to intensify the woodland mood, she stands in the hall to greet arriving party guests. Photograph by Fernando Bengoechea.

For a truly gala small dinner, guests sit under a canopy of Apricot Beauty tulips and aromatic eucalyptus at a table landscaped with books and objects, flowers and candles. It's a lovely way to have all your friends present even for a small dinner. With books by or about them, objects and presents they have given to you, flowers that remind you of them, you may have fifty people in spirit at a dinner for four. The five-branch votive-light candelabra with their central flower containers were designed to be enveloped in foliage—here berried eucalyptus—and they would serve equally well were fifty people present in the flesh at a banquet table. This view from the stairs shows the full complexity of the table arrangement and the variety of objects in silver, porcelain, pottery, stone, and bronze that make it up. The two inlaid chairs against the far wall are Moroccan. Photographs by Guy Lindsay.

199

The dining table is set up parallel to the library table that backs up to the stair rail in a corner of the living room, and both tables are covered to the floor for the evening with aquamarine chintz. The bamboo dining chairs have been given a red jasper painted finish and plump striped cotton cushions. On the library table, padded striped chintz covers a terra-cotta pot containing a phalaenopsis orchid.

Matte gold lacquer place plates, gold-rimmed water goblets, and a gold-leafed bud vase holding a trio of English daisies (*Bellis perennis*) give a soft shimmer to the table and reinforce the warmth of the apricot tulips. A turquoise pottery monkey and a blue-and-white Persian bowl add more tones to the blend of blues in plates, foliage, and cloths. All this may seem a rather extravagant decoration for a small dinner, but one of the great pleasures in entertaining is having the time to think out and put together all of the details that make a happy occasion, whether it is for a few special guests or a large gathering of friends.

Bundles of twiggy branches tied together with raffia spring out of a moss-wrapped metal container to brace a collection of lilies and dendrobium orchids entwined with strands of silver-fleece vine, *Polygonum aubertii*. In the container a clump of delicate yellow orchids is bordered by more lily blooms.

Basket handles provide both frame and support for a flower arrangement. Depending on the materials and the formality or informality of their construction, the handles can also convey a variety of moods. The one thing these handles won't do is allow you to pick up the arrangement. Photographs by Marisa Alvarez Lima.

❧

Another rustic moss basket brims with butterfly weed, *Asclepias tuberosa*, and orange roses. Tucked into its twig handle are sprays of shrubby pink leptospermum.

❧

The container is still moss-bound, but the basket is more controlled and rather oriental in feeling. Four precisely cut twig bundles are tied to the outside of the container to make the uprights and wired together at both ends of the crosspiece. Concealment of the joints offers an excuse for more moss wrappings. Tucked into this miniature bucket a rosebud, a little lily, rose and white freesia, clusters of starry white sedum, and borage buds.

Single flowers, each in a galax-collared glass vase, take their places in a diverse collection assembled on an antique chest of drawers. The stem of glowing 'Enchantment' lilies, the red-and-yellow-striped parrot tulip, the orange ranunculus, and the two pink roses, one deep and one pale, are as much *objets de virtu* as the less ephemeral elements of the composition: boxes in bone, lacquer, porcelain, enamel, wood, silver, and cartonnage; an ivory netsuke; Japanese carved wood toads and monsters in several sizes; a soapstone candleholder; a Thai head and a carved amethyst perfume bottle; a silver basket of potpourri and a tiny flower painting on a tiny bamboo easel. Room decorated by James O'Brien. Photograph by Peter Margonelli.

single flower in a vase of its own really focuses your attention on the special character of *that* flower and, however expert you become at complex arrangements, you will find refreshment for your eye and your imagination by going back from time to time to the simplicity of the single flower. Not that you must be literal about it. Two or three blossoms or stems in a bud vase will serve the same purpose. Single flowers or bud-vase bouquets can also be the building blocks for larger compositions. Simplicity times five or six becomes complex.

A glass garden of single flowers, or so it appears. In fact, each of the chemistry flasks standing in the glass dish with its polished black pebbles holds a small three-level bouquet. From a white freesia cradled in galax, front and center, rise a white rose and a star-of-Bethlehem (*Ornithogalum*) bud. Continuing clockwise, another freesia, two white roses, a spray of yellow oncidium orchids, and plumes of white lilac. At the back, a scarlet nerine flames above a stem of 'Enchantment' lilies. Completing the circle, a spray of white dendrobium orchids, another of oncidium, and a stem of 'Rubrum' speciosum lilies. Photograph by Roger Bester.

A grove of dancing dahlias centers a luncheon table, each stem supported in its crystal flask by a pair of galax leaves. By chance the blooms match almost perfectly the curtains behind them; but a dahlia of any color would be happy with the background in this living room designed by James O'Brien. Photograph by Guy Lindsay.

Between meals, the same dahlias move to an English Regency console with a specimen mineral top and surround an Austrian clock of the same period. Below them is a more permanent bouquet of hydrangeas and over them a contemporary version of a Dutch mirror with an ebony and red tortoiseshell finish. Photograph by Guy Lindsay.

Jovial guardian of the gate, a six-foot teddy bear furred in moss proffers a rosy nosegay to visitors. His chicken-wire frame is stuffed with spaghnum moss and, because of his size, is reinforced with wood. He has lived outside for more than ten years but needs periodic remossing, particularly after a spell of hot, dry weather. Table-size teddy bears, their moss coats bound on with very fine green wire, can have their chicken-wire bodies stuffed with either sphagnum moss or water-retaining foam. There is no end to the animals that can join the moss menagerie and the wire forms sold as foundations for ivy or *ficus pumila* topiaries can easily wear coats of moss instead of growing vines. Photograph by Marisa Alvarez Lima.

❧

Fresh moss, lichens, and dried flowers composed into a subtly colored open heart to hang on a wall or a door. For Valentine's Day, perhaps, but festive at any time, it is made of materials available year round. The dried hydrangeas, rosebuds, bits of saracenia, and toadstools are attached to a chickenwire frame that is both stuffed with and wrapped in moss. Photograph by Marisa Alvarez Lima.

INDEX

Numbers in *italic type* indicate pages on which illustrations occur.

A

achillea, 142
alstroemeria, *139, 156*
amaranth, globe, 156
amaryllis, 18, *19, 75*, 162, 166
amaryllis belladonna, *144*, 145, *152*
anemone, *73*
anthurium, 70
apples, 21, *48–49*, 161, 165, *178–81*
    in fruit pyramid, 161, *177*
Art Deco, 78
artemisia, 175
artichoke, as container, *144–45, 180–81*
asparagus, and flowers, 142, *143*, 145
asparagus fern, *98–99*, 120
    see also sprengeri
aster, 14, 16, *30–31*, 114
    New England, 116
    see also Montecassino aster
Aster novae-belgii, 116
astrantia, red, *144*, 145
autumn flower arrangement, *2, 48–49*
    for wedding, 116, *123*
autumn leaves, 114, 125
azalea, *99*

B

bamboo, 44
    baskets, *156*
    and flower compositions, *88–89,
        182, 183, 188, 189*
    and orchids, *76–77*, 82, *98–99, 194,
        196*, 197
bananas, *103*, 162, *163, 177*
bark, 145
    birch, canister, *148*
baskets, as containers, 36, *37*, 146–50,
    154, 156, 164
    handles, *188, 189, 202–3*
batchelor's buttons, *30–31*

bay, 28, 106, 170
bayberry, *48–49*
beans, 145
    Selma Zebrina, *152, 153*
Bede, the Venerable, 161
Belgian fence espalier, 191
belladonna (amaryllis belladonna), *144,
    145, 152*
Berrall, Julia, 42
berries, 162
birch, 120
    stump pedestal, *197*
    twigs, with flowers, *136–39*
birchbark canister, *148*
birch-branch topiary stems, *24–25, 50,
    184, 185*
bird-of-paradise (strelitzia), *41*
bittersweet, 114, 129, 161
black-eyed Susan, 70, *154*
borage, *203*
boxwood, *99*, 165, 170
    and hydrangea Christmas trees,
        162, *163–64*
    menorah, *174*, 175
    tabletop ornaments, *28–29, 158–59,
        165, 178–79, 186–87*
branches, 20, 38, 100, 145
    downward-curving, 38, *48–49*
    moss-covered, with orchids, *124, 125*
    nailed to tree trunk, *91*
    quince, *88–89*
broccoli, bouquet of, 72
brodiaea, *113, 139, 141, 195*
Brodiaea laxa, 182, 183
brunia, silver, *178–79*
bud-vase bouquets, 16, *73, 201, 205*
buffet table, 60, 95, 101
    decorations for, *72–73, 103*
    in tent, 101, 137
butterfly weed (*Asclepias tuberosa*), *203*

C

cabbage, 72
calendula, 192, *193*
camellia, 116, 170

Campbell, Joseph, 170
candelabra
    electrified, in tent, *138*
    garlanded, for church wedding,
        130–3
    of votive lights, 60, *61, 198–99*
candles, 69, 70
    votive, 32, *33, 58–61*, 69, *75, 86–89,
        108–9*, 142, *143*, 170, *171, 174,
        175, 180–81, 186–87, 198–99*
cantaloupe, as container, 145
carnation, 21, 42, 65, 67, 117
caspia (*Limonium bellidifolium*), *27*
castor oil plant (*Ricinus communis*), 11
cauliflower, bouquet of, *72*
cedar wreath, feathery, *173*
celosia, wheat, 156, *157*
Celosia cristata, see cockscomb
chard, *72*, 145
cherries, Spanish, *20*
cherry blossoms, 38
Chinese lantern (*Physalis franchetii*),
    calyxes of, 162, *163*
Christmas decorations, 158–70
    local plants, 175
    tabletop ornaments, 162, *167*, 170,
        171, 176, 178–79
    trees, planted, *168, 169*
    wreaths and garlands, 170, *172–73,*
        175
church wedding, decorations for, 104,
    105, 119, *110–11, 128–35*
cinnamon, 21, 161, 172, *178–79*
clivia, *73*
cockscomb (*Celosia cristata*), 18, *19,
    24–25*, 42, *148*
Congea tomentosa, 124
containers
    bamboo, *156*
    crystal, *145*
    disposable, 127
    fabric-covered, 192, *193–95*
    flower stems in, 142, *190–91*
    fruits and vegetables as, *64–65,
        144–45, 180–81*
    moss-covered, *27, 108*, 146, *147, 184,
        185, 202–3*

and natural elements, 145–46, 150
  relation of flowers to, 38, 44
  for single flowers, 36, 44, *204–5*
cornflower, *70–71, 118*, 150, *151*
cosmos, red, 118
cotoneaster, 170
country club parties, 78, 100
chuppah, 120, *121*

D

dahlia, 22, *23, 48–49, 75, 206–7*
daisy, *28, 64,* 65, 70, 118, 165
  African, 192, *193*
  English (*Bellis perennis*), *201*
  Michaelmas, 114, 116
  Shasta, *85, 88–89*
dance floor, 91, 97, 101, 137
delphinium, 11, 22, *23, 73*
didiscus, *68*
dining table decorations
  centerpiece, 58–60, 65, 67
  lighting, 69–70, 83
  outdoor, 70
  in tent, *140–41*
  on terrace, *64,* 65, 70, *125*
  see also buffet table; table settings
dogwood, 22, 38, 54
dried flower arrangements, *26–27*
dusty miller, 175

E

eggplant, *20, 144,* 145
entertaining, planning for, 65–66, 83–84
eremurus (foxtail lilies), *45,* 50, *51*
erigeron (fleabane), *154*
eucalyptus, *48–49, 54–55,* 91, *155, 172, 198–200*
euonymous, 170
euphorbia (*Euphorbia palustris*), 22, *23*
Euphorbia fulgens, 38
evergreens, 170
evergreen wreaths, *173*

F

fabric-covered containers, 192, *195*
Fatsia japonica, 11
ferns, *52,* 104, *105, 110–11, 128–29,* 127
  asparagus, *98–99, 110*
  Boston, *110*
  see also sprengeri
ficus trees, *94,* 95
fleabane (erigeron), *154*
flower, single, 16, 36, 44, *204–5*
flower paintings, 38–42, 146
flowers, conditioning of, 22–24
flower stems, cutting, 22, 28, 46
  poppies, 36
forget-me-not, 155
forsythia, 20, 22, 38
fountain grass (pennisetum), 14, *15*
foxtail lilies, *see* eremurus
fragrance, *see* scent
freesia, 21, 38, *190,* 205
  in mixed arrangements, *12,* 16, *17, 26–27, 62–63,* 67, 68, *87, 149, 156, 188,* 189, *195, 203*
  in wedding bouquets and decorations, *108, 113, 117, 122–23, 131, 134, 139, 141*
fruit, *20,* 21, *73,* 161
  as container, 145
  in pyramids, 97, 161, *177*
  see also apples; grapes; pineapple; strawberries; watermelon
fuchsia, 38

G

galax leaves, 10-11, *28, 32, 35, 40, 45, 53,* 58, *59, 72, 87, 93, 95, 148, 149, 153, 177, 205, 206–7*
  artificial, *186–87*
  on candles, *32, 33,* 58, *59, 88–89, 112–13*
  on containers, 28, *29, 141, 152, 196, 197, 204*

in wedding bouquets and decorations, *108, 115, 118, 122–23, 130–35*
gardenia, 21, 65, 116
garlands
  Christmas, 170, 175
  of ferns, 104, *105,* 127
  on lighting fixtures, 8, *9,* 96
  of sprengeri, *80–81, 92–93,* 96, *102–3,* 197
  wedding, *110–11, 130–33*
geranium leaves, 11
gerbera, *27, 91, 98–99, 110, 129, 139*
ginger, flowering, 21, 70
gladiolus, *57*
Glastonbury thorn, 166
godetia, 10, *68,* 118, *195*
goldenrod, 10, 16, *30–31*
gomphrena, 156
grapes, *20, 103,* 177
  and flowers, 22, *23,* 28, *29, 50, 93, 149*
grapevines, *72, 149*
  dried, *98–99*
grass, pampas, 21
grasses, 10, 14, 145, 175
  dried, 177
greens, *see* evergreens; vegetable foliage

H

Hanukkah, 175
hay Christmas trees, tabletop, *176*
heather, 16, 170
  Hanukkah decoration, *174,* 175
  white, holiday wreath, *173*
hedges, 100, *186–87*
herbs, 21, 106, 170
  see also bay; rosemary
hibiscus, 70
holly, 170
horsetail, equisetum, 156, *157*
hosta, 11
House of the Americas, patio, *102–3*
hyacinth, 21, *62–63,* 65, 67, *87, 149, 156,* 166, 192, *193*

and asparagus container, 142, *143*
in basket composition, 146, *147*
in wedding bouquets and decorations,
    117, 118, 131, 134
hydrangea, 28, *29, 48–49, 50,* 70, *71, 72,*
    152, 207
and boxwood trees, 162, *164*
dried, *209*
Pee Gee (*Hydrangea paniculata*
    'Grandiflora'), *26–27, 54–55,*
    162, *163*
stem of, 142

I

Ingres, Jean-Auguste-Dominique, 83
iris, 38, 166
ivy, *116,* 119, *177*
ixia, 50, *51,* 58, *59*
ixora, scarlet, *32*

J

jasmine, 21, 65
Jewish wedding decorations, 118
juniper, *168,* 169, 170
    sprigs, on menorah, 175

K

kale, *72*
kalmia, 170

L

lace flower
    blue (*Trachymene coerulea*),
        36, 37, 52, 56
    in wedding bouquets and decorations,
        117, 118, 131, 134
    white, *180–81*
lady's-slipper, *194*
lavender, 21, 28, 113
    dried, *155*

leaves, 10–11, 44, 145
    autumn, 129
    bouquet of, 21
    removing from stems, 24, 56
    see also galax leaves
leptospermum, *203*
lettuce, 72
lichen, 99, 145, *209*
lighting, 69–70, 82–83, 97
    fixtures, decorated, 8, *9, 90, 124, 138*
    see also candelabra; candles
lilac, 20, 21, 22, 54, *205*
    in mixed bouquets, 18, *19,* 50, *51, 56,*
        85, 87, 88, *89, 117*
lily, 16, 20, 21, *32,* 38, 104, 166
    in artichoke container, *144–45*
    and bamboo compositions, *76–77,*
        88–89, 98–99
    'Casa Blanca,' *48–49, 149*
    'Enchantment,' *204, 205*
    hybrid, *54–55,* 57
    miniature, *156*
    in mixed arrangements, 14, *15,*
        26–31, 34, 62–63, 84–85, 87, 91,
        112–13, 152, 156, 192, 193, 195,
        202, 203
    orange, *72, 96*
    'Pink Glory,' *40*
    Rothschild, *53,* 129
    rubrum, *80–81, 85, 205*
    speciosum, *88–89, 205*
    'Stargazer,' *118, 131, 134*
    in wedding bouquets and decorations,
        110, 117, 118, 129, 132, 134, 141
lily of the valley, *42,* 69, *149,* 166
    in wedding bouquets and decorations,
        104, 106, *108, 117, 122–23, 141*
lisianthus, 10, 38, *39, 48–49, 117, 131,*
    134, 156

M

maiden grass (*Miscanthus sinensis*
    'Gracillimus'), *177*
maple leaves, scarlet, 20
marigold, 42

menorah, *174,* 175
Metropolitan Museum of Art
    Blumenthal Patio, *78–81, 84–85*
    Temple of Dendur, *86–89*
Mies van der Rohe, Ludwig, 82
mock orange, 22
Monstera deliciosa, 98–99
Montecassino aster (September weed),
    10, 14, *15,* 120
moss, *41,* 44, *53, 149*
    as concealment, *52, 103, 128, 139,*
        146, *147, 154, 172, 176, 196, 197*
    and dried roses, *42, 43, 160,* 166, *167,*
        170, *171,* 184, *185*
    and hay Christmas tree, *176*
    heart-shaped composition, *209*
    and orchids, *103, 124–25*
    on pedestals, 99, *197*
    sphagnum, *99,* 146, *147, 208*
    teddy bear, 170, *171, 208*
    see also oakmoss; Spanish moss
moss-covered containers, 27, *112,*
    146, *147, 202–3*
    terra cotta, 145–46, 184, *185*
museum halls, decoration of, 78
    see also Metropolitan Museum of Art
myrtle, Swedish, 28

N

narcissus, 21, 65, *67, 155,* 162, *163,* 166,
    168, 169, *188,* 189
nasturtium, 65
nerine, 16, *17,* 34, *35,* 40, 50, *67,* 72,
    139, 205
    in bridal bouquets, *116,* 120, *121*
Nerine sarniensis, 40
nicotiana, 155
nosegays, 42, 58, *59,* 106, *107,* 118, *132,*
    144, 145, *153, 156, 208*
nuts, 161, 165

O

oakmoss, *40*
olive branchlets, on menorah, 175

oranges, 21, *103*, 161
orchid
   and bamboo arrangements, *76–77,*
      82, 98–99, 194, 196, 197
   in big bouquets, *84–85, 88–89*
   chartreuse cymbidium, *96*
   dendrobium, *26–27, 32,* 48, *49,* 60,
      61, *80–81, 110, 115,* 158, *159,*
      196, 197, *202, 205*
   mahogany cypripedium, *32*
   oncidium, *98–99, 102–3, 205*
   phalaenopsis, *201*
   in wedding decorations, *110, 129,*
      124–25, 132, 133, 135, 139
   yellow, *202, 205*
Organization of American States, 102

P

palm
   leaf fan, *41, 45*
   phoenix, *73*
   trees, 82, *87, 102–3*
palmetto leaves, *88–89, 196–97*
pampas grass, 21
parfums d'ambiance, 21–22
parties, planning for, 65–66, 83, 90
passiflora, 119
peaches, 161
pears, 161, *177*
pennisetum (fountain grass), 14, *15*
peony, 16, *20,* 21, 76, *77*
   and lilacs, *56*
   in mixed bouquets, 28, *34,* 54, *58, 59,*
      108–9, 195
   in wedding bouquets, *117, 118*
petunia, 65, 70
phlox, 65
pieris, 170
pineapple, *103,* 145, *177*
   miniature, *74, 75*
pineapple flower (*Eucomis autumnalis*),
   30–31
pittosporum, 170
plumbago, 70

plumeria, 70
poinsettia, 162–66
pomanders, 161
pomegranates, 161
poppy, *36–37, 62–63,* 118
   California (*Eschscholzia*), *52*
   cutting and treatment of, 36
   Iceland, *52, 95*
posy, *12, 40, 68,* 104
potpourri, 21–22, *32,* 172, *204–5*
prickly pears, *20*
primrose, *188,* 189
Proust, Marcel, 189
pyramidal wire forms, 161

Q

Queen Anne's lace, 21, 65, 70, 170, *171*
   in garlands, *131,* 132, *133*
   in mixed bouquets, *12,* 50, *51, 57, 68,*
      118, 149
quince branches, *20,* 22, 38, *88–89*

R

raffia, 44
   and bamboo, *188,* 189, *196, 197*
   tassels, *45*
   ties and bows, *40, 41, 53, 118, 141,*
      144–45, 150, *151, 156, 176,*
      190–94, 202
ranunculus, 50, *51, 62–63, 75, 131, 134,*
   149, 188, 189, *204*
reeds, *20–21,* 145
restaurant, entertaining in, 90
   Le Cirque, *94–96*
rhododendron, 170
Ricinus communis, 11
rose, 21, *40, 42, 43,* 54, 70, 142
   buds, 34, *35, 52,* 104, *168, 169, 203*
   buds, dried, 27, *42, 43,* 162, *164,*
      170–72, 176, 184, *185, 209*
   Christmas (*Helleborus niger*), *149*

   in Christmas wreath, *172*
   dried, *160, 164,* 166, *167, 176*
   Fire and Ice, *93*
   floribunda, 50, *51,* 54, *197*
   in garlands, *96*
   and grapes, *93*
   miniature, *34*
   in mixed arrangements, *12,* 28–31,
      34–37, 48–51, *62–63,* 67, 68, *72,*
      73, 149, *152,* 192, *193, 195, 203,*
      205
   in nosegays, *106, 107, 118, 144, 145,*
      153, 156, 208
   polyantha, *30–31*
   single, 16, 184, *185, 190,* 204
   tea, *34,* 50, *51,* 54
   in wedding bouquets and decorations,
      106, 107, 113, 117, 118, 131,
      132–34
rosemary, 28, *106,* 170, 175
rudbeckias, double, *154*

S

santolina, 175
saracenia, *209*
Saturnalia, 161–62
scabiosa, 28, *29, 152*
scallions, *153*
scent, 21–22, 161, 172
   dining with perfumed flowers, 65
sedum, *72, 203*
   Autumn Joy, *153*
September weed, *see* Montecassino
   aster
single flower, 16, 36, 44, *204, 205*
smilax, 60, *61,* 119, *130–33*
snapdragon, *57*
Snyder, Phillip V., 166
Spanish moss, *45, 80–81, 85, 98–99,*
   88–89, 102–3, 177, 190
sphagnum moss, *93,* 146, *147, 208*
sprengeri, *84–85, 91–93, 96, 102–3,*
   119, *197*
spring flowers, 54, 162–66

spruce, 170

squash, 72

   as container, *144*, 145

star-of-Bethlehem, *32*, *191*, *205*

statice, 161

stephanotis, 21, *116*

steps, lighting of, 97

stock, 21, *139*

strawberries, and flowers, 32, *33*

strelitzia (bird-of-paradise), *41*

summer flower arrangements, *54*, *56*,
   64, 65

   wedding bouquet, *118*

sunflower, 10, 38, 129

sweet pea, 10, 16, *32*, *33*

   in mixed arrangements, *12*, *28–29*,
     34, 36, *37*, *58*, *59*, *62–63*, 68, *153*,
     195

   in wedding bouquets and decorations,
     116–18, *130–31*, 134

sweet sultan, *52*, *56*

T

table settings

   holiday festivity, 158, *159*, *180–81*

   home dining, *58–59*, *62–63*, *74–75*,
     186–87, 196, 197, *198–201*

   large party, *88*, *92–95*, *180–81*

   lunch, *64*, 65, 67, *69*, 70, *71*, *74*, *75*,
     206–7

   reception, *112*, 13

   and size of table, 97

   see also buffet table; dining table
     decorations

teddy bear, moss-coated, 170, *171*, *208*

tents, decoration of, 97–101, *124*,
   136–41

   trees in, 100, 120

Thanksgiving, 158–61

   table ornaments, *165*, 177

toadstools, 146, *147*, *209*

topiary work, *24–25*, 42, *43*, *50*, 100,
   158, *159*, 170, *171*, 182, 184, *187*, 208

trees and boughs, 22, 120

Christmas, 166–70

ficus, *94*, 95

   palm, 82, *87*, *102–3*

   in tents, 100, 120

   see also branches; twigs

tuberose, 116

tulip, 14–16, 142, 166, 170, *171*

   Apricot Beauty, *198–201*

   buds, parrot, *62–63*, *75*

   double, *73*

   Estrella Rynveld parrot, *50*, *51*

   Flaming Parrot, *18*

   in garlands, *96*

   lily-flowered, 54, 76

   in mixed arrangements, *18*, *19*, 50, *51*,
     58, *59*, *73*

   in wedding decorations, *129*, *141*

   yellow-striped parrot, *204*

tussie-mussie, 34, *35*, 67, *118*

twigs, *141*, 145

   as basket handles, *202–3*

   birch, with flowers, *136–39*

   in chuppah, 120

   holly, 170

V

vegetable foliage, *72*

vegetables, as containers, *144–45*

   see also artichoke; asparagus; beans;
     scallions

verbena, lemon, 28

veronica, 16, *17*

Versailles box, 16, *17*, 28, *29*, *50*, 67,
   166, *167*, *186–87*

vetiver root, 172

viburnum, 18, *19*, *67*, 111

   corymbs, *62–63*

   snowball, 192, *193*

vines, 60, 119, 175

   Congea tomentosa, *124*

   silver-fleece (*Polygonum aubertii*), *202*

   see also ivy; sprengeri

violets, 16, 118

votive lights, *see* candles

W

watercress, 72

water lily (*Victoria amazonica*), 86

watermelon, as container, *64*, 65, 145

weddings

   bride's bouquet, *104–8*, *115–18*,
     120–21, *123*, 130

   bride's dress, 114

   chuppah, 120, *121*

   church decorations, 104, *105*, 119,
     110–11, *129*, *130–35*

   photographer, 127

   planning, 109, 114, 126

   reception, *112*, 113, *124–27*,
     136–141

   seasonal flowers, 114, *116*, *118*, 129

wheat, *30–31*, 145, 150, *151*, 161, 175

   in wedding bouquets, 106, 114, *116*,
     118

wheat celosia, 156, *157*

wildflowers, 10, 106, 154

winter flower arrangements, *26–27*, *155*

wisteria, 38

wreaths, 170, *172–73*, 175

Y

yew, 170, *173*

Z

zinnia, 20, 65